ETHICAL THEORY

ETHICAL THEORY

in the last quarter of
the twentieth century

Edited, with Introduction, by
NORMAN E. BOWIE

CHARLES L. STEVENSON

WILLIAM K. FRANKENA

R. B. BRANDT

A. I. MELDEN

HACKETT PUBLISHING COMPANY
Indianapolis / Cambridge

239536

Interior design by James N. Rogers

Printed in the United States of America

First printing

For further information, please address
Hackett Publishing Company, Inc.
Box 44937, Indianapolis, IN 46204

Library of Congress Cataloging in Publication Data
Main entry under title:

Ethical theory in the last quarter of the twentieth century.

Includes index.
1. Ethics—Addresses, essays, lectures. I. Melden,
A. I. (Abraham Irving), 1910–   . II. Bowie,
Norman E., 1942–

BJ1012.E884	170	82–1006
ISBN 0–915145–34–0		AACR2

The paper in this book meets the guidelines for permanence and durability established by the Committee on Production Guidelines for Book Longevity of the Council on Library Resources.

to the memory of
CHARLES L. STEVENSON

CONTENTS

Preface

As logic and epistemology dominated the first half of twentieth-century philosophy, ethics dominates its last half. The shift in emphasis is largely due to the work of American ethicists who responded to the analytic revolution in philosophy by attempting to find a legitimate place for ethics in the philosophical landscape.

Three philosophers who became colleagues at the University of Michigan contributed greatly to that effort. Professor Charles Stevenson attempted an analysis of ethical language which both captured what is unique about ethical language and attempted to show how reasoning about ethical judgments can take place. Professor William Frankena developed a careful analysis which distinguished the moral point of view from other points of view and discussed various other questions about it. In the meantime, Professor Richard Brandt pioneered efforts to revitalize and defend the theory of utilitarianism which had fallen into decline as the result of attacks on Bentham, Mill, and Sidgwick. On the west coast, Professor A. I. Melden revitalized the natural rights tradition, so central to the political philosophy of the founding fathers. Melden focused on the act of promise-keeping and argued that the concept of a right was necessary to fully understand the ethical nature of promises.

During the 1977-79 academic years, the University of Delaware honored these four distinguished philosophers for their contributions to ethics. This volume contains the mature reflections of these philosophers, who raised issues in meta-ethical theory which set the tone for debate in the last half of the twentieth century. The dedicatee is Charles Stevenson, whose untimely death occurred before the series was completed. The Center for the Study of Values acknowledges with deep appreciation a grant from the Matchette Foundation which made the lecture series possible. The editor acknowledges with equal appreciation the secretarial support of Mrs. Sandy Manno which helped make this volume possible.

Introduction

Writing from the perspective of the early 1980s, it is hard to imagine the dismay that the logical positivism of the 1940s caused for many philosophers pursuing ethics. A. J. Ayer's *Language Truth and Logic* seemed to reduce ethics to emotional ejaculations—e.g., Good, Hurrah! The response of many philosophers to positivists like Ayer was as emotional as the positivists' theory indicated. This hostility was also directed against Charles Stevenson's *Ethics and Language*. Seldom was hostility more misplaced. Stevenson's enterprise was to show that acceptance of a type of emotivism in ethics was not inconsistent with a view of ethics as rational discourse. On Stevenson's account, if I say that tolerance is good I am approving of tolerance and inviting you to do so as well. Suppose you disagree with me. Stevenson would say that you do not share my attitude about tolerance. To effect a change in your attitude I would marshal a set of factors which would provide reasons for you to join me in approving of tolerance.

One of the major objections to Stevenson's view was that he had no way to distinguish good reasons from bad ones. Some critics argued that anything could count as a reason as long as it brought about the desired change in attitude. From the beginning Stevenson thought this criticism reflected a misunderstanding of his work and that it was wrong on its own merits. He distinguished between descriptive meaning and emotive meaning and between propaganda and rational persuasion. There are both rational and nonrational means for effecting a change in attitude.

Before Stevenson's response to his critics was well known and understood, an alternative theory of the role of reason in ethics captured a wide philosophical audience. This alternative was most carefully developed in R. M. Hare's *Freedom and Reason*. For Hare, rationality in ethical discourse is required by the principle of universalizability—a principle which is logical in nature rather than moral. If an agent calls something good in one case, that agent must be committed to calling it good in similar cases: a reason in one case must be a reason in all similar cases. It is this requirement of universalizability which Hare believes we can use to show almost anyone who thinks it morally permissible to gas Jews that he is rationally mistaken.

In the paper for this volume Charles Stevenson denies that Hare provides a better account of the place of reason in ethics than he does. In his paper, Stevenson accepts as correct Sidgwick's principle:

> If I judge any action to be right for myself, I implicitly judge it to be right for any other person whose nature and circumstances do not differ from mine in certain important respects.

Such a principle rules out any exclusively self-excepting statement such as "It is right for me to steal but not right for others to steal—no matter how closely their circumstances resemble mine."

First Stevenson shows how his emotive theory of ethics accommodates Sidgwick's principle. Recall that on Stevenson's view, to say that something is good is to approve it and to invite others to approve it as well. But surely any judgment which violates Sidgwick's principle, e.g., a solely self-exclusionary one, would be a pointless invitation. Why would anyone else join you in approving it? Indeed, such solely self-exclusionary judgments are so pointless, Stevenson observes, that we do not even find them in diaries.

Stevenson is now ready to expand his analysis to a principle of his own: "the principle of implicit generality." According to this principle, when anyone makes a judgment, that person is committed to a judgment that is explicitly general and nonsingularizing, together with the claim that the initial judgment is a special case of it. To explain Stevenson's principle, a singularizing property must be defined: "A property is singularizing just in case it can be designated only with the help of a singular term—only with the help of a proper name or a surrogate of a proper name." A few of Stevenson's examples make his point clear:

1. "When a man says, 'Jones's act was praiseworthy' he is thereby committed to this further assertion: 'There is some [perhaps highly complex] factual property, P, which satisfies the following conditions: (1) P is non-singularizing and (2) Jones's act had P, and (3) Every act that has P is praiseworthy.

2. "When a man says, 'Jane ought to be pensioned' he is
    committed to this further assertion: 'Jane has some factual
    and non-singularizing property, P, such that anyone who
    has P ought to be pensioned.'"

Stevenson then goes on to defend his principle of implicit
generality in the same way he defended Sidgwick's. In the process of making the defense, he shows how judgments based on
the exclusive loyalty to a group can be rejected, e.g., "The
citizens of Fairhaven ought to be exempted from taxes, even
though they have no factual and singularizing property, P, such
that everyone having P ought to be exempted from taxes." Indeed, Stevenson even thinks his analysis will show that
judgments by nation-states which violate his principle will be rejected as well.

Now there are obvious parallels between Stevenson's principle of implicit generality and R. M. Hare's principle of universalizability. Hare, as you may recall, builds his principle of
universalizability into the meaning of a moral judgment. In the
latter part of his paper, Stevenson asks whether his principle
should be similarly construed as analytically a priori. His
answer is provocative: "As I see it, the question can be answered
by a flip of a coin." The reason for his answer is that building
his principle into the meaning of value judgments "simply gives
a linguistic turn to a rule that arises from people's purposes in
judging—a rule that they will follow whether they consider it
linguistic or not." The basic sanction for violation of the principle is psychological, not linguistic. In this regard Stevenson
diverges from Hare in one of two ways. Hare adds universalizability to his prescriptivism and hence either underestimates
the power of prescriptivism because he fails to realize that
prescriptivism with its psychological background is sufficient to
show that violations of universalizability are pointless—or he is
overestimating the power of universalizability because he is
building universalizability into the language in a preemptive
way.

Stevenson's discussion of what should and what should not
be built into the definition of a value judgment is but one act in
a larger play. That larger play has as its theme the question,
"What does it mean to take the moral point of view?"

Graduate students in the 1960s became familiar with the
problems raised in defining the moral point of view when they
agonized about Hare's fanatic. If the average person asking

whether or not he should send Jews to the gas chamber were confronted with Hare's universalizability test, he would say No because he would be unwilling to go to the gas chamber if he were a Jew. But what about the consistent Jew-hater—the one willing to go to the gas chamber if he were a Jew? On Hare's criteria it appears as if he would be counted as taking the moral point of view since he is willing to both prescribe and universalize his moral judgments. But somehow most of us rebel at the thought of a fanatic Jew-hater as being moral—and our rebellion cannot be explained simply by the fact that the content of his moral opinions just happens to differ from ours.

One way to look at this question is to ask, "What does it mean to take the moral point of view?" This question represents the focus of William Frankena's paper, "Moral Point of View Theories." What makes the moral point of view concept so rich is that so many theorists have used the concept to assist in resolving meta-ethical issues. Frankena identifies four tasks which have engaged the attention of moral-point-of-view theorists: (1) that of defining morality or marking the distinction between the moral and the nonmoral; (2) that of formulating and establishing a test for determining which moral judgments and norms are true, valid, or at least justified; (3) that of seeing what animates morality or makes it tick; and (4) that of showing why we should be moral.

But what do all moral-point-of-view theorists have in common? Frankena identifies four theses which, he believes, nearly all such theorists share:

A. There is such a thing as a single, distinct, and definable point of view which may appropriately be called *the* moral point of view and which is the view taken when we try to formulate our most basic moral obligations.

B. We should distinguish the moral from the nonmoral by a direct or indirect reference to the moral point of view.

C. Basic moral judgments are true, valid, or at least rationally justified if they are conceived from the moral point of view and after a clear-headed and full review of all that is relevant.

D. We should take the moral point of view.

What divides moral-point-of-view theorists? Frankena catalogues many of the issues that divide them, but in his discussion of Baier and Taylor, he identifies the issue which has become the most known and discussed—should one build consideration of others into the definition of the moral point of view? In the literature this issue has become known as the dispute between the formalists and the materialists. Frankena, although a materialist himself, accepts Taylor's criticism that Baier is guilty of ethnocentrism when he builds the equal consideration of interests into his definitions of the moral point of view. Moreover, Frankena finds Taylor equally guilty of ruling out castes and slavery from moral discussions. What distinguishes Frankena and Taylor here is the notion of equality. Frankena argues that taking the moral point of view involves having respect for all consciously sentient beings capable of suffering—but not necessarily *equal* respect.

The discussion of the formalist-materialist dispute provides a bridge for considering debates from within the fraternity to attacks from without. Alan Gewirth agrees with Frankena that one ought to take the interests of others into account, but he disagrees with Frankena that the best justification for such a principle is provided by the concept of the moral point of view. Rather than criticize Gewirth's alternative theory, Frankena defends his own moral point of view theory against Gewirth's criticisms. Although Frankena concedes that some of Gewirth's criticisms are effective against other moral-point-of-view-theorists, he denies that those criticisms apply to his own theory. Frankena believes that Gewirth's greatest challenge is found in Gewirth's criticism that the concept of a moral point of view cannot explain why we should be moral. Frankena emphasizes that the moral-point-of-view theorist is not stuck with merely hypothetical imperatives of the form "If and only if you take the moral point of view, then you ought to do so and so." Basic moral oughts are categorical in the sense that they apply irrespective of the agent's inclinations, interests, or point of view. Of course, that doesn't show that a person *actually* is bound by the perspective of the moral point of view—but what theory could show that?

Frankena then turns to his most recent formulation of the moral point of view. Although the moral point of view should be neutral, it should indicate the kinds of considerations, facts, or reasons relevant in the making of moral judgments. Such facts are those about the impact that acts, agents, traits, and so forth have on conscious sentient beings including, but not limited to, the agent in question. Frankena defends himself against the ethnocentric critic by arguing that he indicates only what sorts of facts are relevant; he "does not say *which* facts are relevant in *which* way to *which* judgments." In doing this one does not adopt any specific moral view. However, taking the moral point of view is not simply accepting and using certain sorts of facts as reasons for moral judgments. Rather, the moral point of view is the source for taking those facts as relevant. This source is then identified in psychological terms as "a Caring or Non-Indifference about what happens to persons and conscious, sentient beings." In taking the moral point of view when we make moral judgments, we are not simply inviting others to do likewise, as Stevenson would. Rather, we are claiming that all others who take the moral point of view and are fully rational will agree with us, and moreover that for basic moral judgments such a claim is true. Of course the moral-point-of-view theorist cannot prove that it is rational to take the moral-point-of-view—but if such a question of choice were given to a free, clearheaded, logical person with a vivid imagination and complete self-knowledge coupled with complete knowledge of the world, that person would answer in favor of the moral point of view. Frankena concludes his essay by raising a troublesome problem: Would a person who simply loved conscious sentient beings without attributing rights to them or conceiving oneself as having duties to them, be operating from the moral point of view?

If one believes that taking the moral point of view includes taking the interests of others into account, a long tradition in ethics describes how this ought to be done; that tradition is utilitarianism. Despite utilitarianism's long history and great vitality, it did not fare well in America during the first half of the twentieth century—for American ethics was then dominated by pragmatism, the self-realization ethics of personalism, and Roycean idealism. When American philosophers discussed utilitarianism, their example of a recent utilitarian was Mill. Now, American philosophers cite Richard Brandt as the contemporary utilitarian.

Brandt's great contribution to utilitarian thought was to provide it with more sophistication, and I don't mean the sophistication of decision theory. Rather, Brandt combined conceptual analysis with the latest empirical findings of psychology. Traditional criticisms of utilitarianism focused on its inadequate treatment of rules, its lack of concern with motives, its inability to measure, and its easy vulnerability to counterexamples based on justice. Brandt believed that utilitarianism was capable of being formulated in ways which enabled it to give an account of all the concerns of traditional ethics and to do so in a way far more plausible than any of its competitors. His paper "Problems of Contemporary Utilitarianism: Real and Alleged" represents his most recent defense of the utilitarian tradition.

Brandt is a rule utilitarian. He begins his paper by putting his own theory into historical perspective. Contrary to the conventional wisdom which views rule utilitarianism as evolving from the ashes of critiques of act utilitarianism, Brandt finds antecedents of rule utilitarianism in such unlikely places as Epicurus, St. Thomas, and Bishop Berkeley.

Brandt then begins his substantive explanation of utilitarianism—an explanation grounded in anthropology and psychology. He begins with the morality of society and more particularly with the consciences of the individuals of society. Rather than ignore motivation, Brandt takes conscience as central. People in society have certain aversions to doing things; they disapprove of others when they do these things; they will feel guilt when they do these things themselves; and they will develop a set of acceptable excuses for certain types of infractions. The morality of the society is represented by the morality of the individual members of the society: "the conscience of the average man or something like that."

But is the morality of society right (correct)? Brandt's rule utilitarianism has a standard for answering that question. The morally superior societal moral code is the optimal code for that society and the optimal code is the one that maximizes welfare. However, in considering whether or not the code maximizes welfare, one must consider whether the code is widely adopted or not, whether it is difficult to teach, and the impact of living with the type of conscience the code requires. Brandt defines a rule-utilitarian "as a person who thinks that what is right or wrong morally is identified by the content of an 'optimal' moral code for the agent's society."

Brandt then addresses the various problems which afflict, and some of the criticisms leveled against, this version of rule utilitarianism. First, what should an American consider as her society—the state in which she resides, the U.S. as a whole, or the American Bar Association of which she is a member? A rule-utilitarian should recognize that these special institutions may require special codes. Indeed, the formulation of such codes is at least part of the domain of professional ethics. Utilitarians must give further thought as to whether the moral code of a professional can direct a professional to do something which in the same situation society would not permit. Utilitarians must also think more about what moral characteristics they should ascribe to such quasipersons as corporations or governments.

Brandt enters the debate that goes back to Bentham and Mill: What is the relationship between utilitarianism and hedonism? Logically, utilitarianism is independent of any concept of the good. However, Brandt's remarks indicate that hedonism has a stronger case than is traditionally thought. He adopts the motivational theory of pleasure. In this theory some element of experience is pleasurable if the person wants to continue or repeat it for itself and not for extraneous reasons. On this view, more than mere physical sensations are pleasant, and hedonistic utilitarianism is not so narrow as some critics have thought. On the motivational theory of pleasure, reading a book, solving a crossword puzzle, or writing a philosophy paper are all pleasurable experiences.

Another standard critique of all forms of utilitarianism is that it cannot resolve the measurability problem. Brandt believes that pleasurable experiences are measurable in terms of hedon-moments and that we can speak of the net balance of hedon-moments. Rather than debate the merits of hedon-moments, Brandt confronts the implications of his view. Should we have many people less happy or fewer people more happy? He considers the various rules society could adopt. What about a moral requirement that a couple have a child if it were reasonable to expect that the child would be happy? Brandt presents conclusive evidence that such a rule would not be optimal in the manner previously specified. Rule utilitarianism is not in logical opposition to efforts at population control.

What about discounting the future? It seems that the hedon-moments of future generations should count as much as the hedon-moments of present persons, and that the hedon-moments of animals should count as much as those of humans (much more than they do now). Brandt argues that some discounting is surely permitted because rule utilitarianism is committed to *expectable* utility, and surely the happiness of both future generations and animals is more speculative than the happiness of present persons. However, for Brandt that is all that is needed in terms of a discount. After that, the interests of future generations and animals do count equally.

Is there a greater obligation to avoid harm than to do good? Many, including so-called negative utilitarians, argue that there is. Brandt agrees with these persons and believes that his own criteria for determining optimal rules will establish the priority of avoiding harm.

A common philosophical objection to rule utilitarianism is that it is utopian. Critics holding this opinion doubt that a society can, without being counterproductive, evaluate acts by the optimal code when a less-than-optimal code is currently in effect. The clash between the two codes would make the optimal code no longer optimal. On conceptual or empirical grounds Brandt refutes three variations of this general criticism.

Finally, Brandt turns to the old "bugaboo" —the charge that utilitarianism permits injustice, particularly on the ground that utilitarianism permits too much inequality. On grounds of both fact and theory, Brandt thinks his critics are mistaken.

Using the tools of philosophical analysis as well as insights from psychology, anthropology, and economics, Brandt enriched one of the fundamental and widely accepted theories of ethics. About the same time a similar enrichment of a central but very different ethical theory took place.

Perhaps the most neglected moral concept in the first six decades of the twentieth century was the concept of a "moral right." "Rights" were prominent in the vocabulary of politicians and statesmen, as in the U. N. Declaration of Human Rights; yet the word was not prominent in the vocabulary of philosophers. Those of us who write on matters of ethics in the 1980s are struck by the contrast. The word "right" is a central concept in discussions of ethical matters. In the latter quarter of the twentieth century, we are indeed taking rights seriously. Professor A. I. Melden's contribution to moral philosophy is that he took rights seriously when few others were prepared to do so. His arguments that such fundamental ethical actions as promise keeping could only be *fully* explained by making use of the concept of moral rights reached its full development in *Rights and Persons* (1977). In the paper "On Moral Rights" for this volume, Melden continues that analysis. He begins by showing how such classical philosophers as Kant, Hobbes, and Locke, as well as twentieth-century writers such as Prichard and Ross, provide a restricted and narrow view of moral duty. These philosophers neglected the fact that the notion of moral duty is inextricably tied to the notion of moral rights. After all, what is wrong with breaking a promise? To break a promise is to interfere with the promisee's endeavor and hence to violate his/her agency. But describing promise-breaking in that way is what one means by violating one's rights. To recognize someone as an agent is to recognize that person as a rights-bearer—and to recognize that person as a rights-bearer is to take his/her interests seriously.

Establishing the relation between being an agent and being a rights-bearer aids in understanding Melden's view that the significant data for ethics are human actions and interactions. Indeed, Melden is then able to enrich the traditional notion of a promise by including the concept of a right and the concern for the interests of the rights-bearer which the notion of a right implies. "Why, then, should he [the promiser] as the reasonable and conscientious agent he is, adjust his own affairs and stay ready to meet his obligations [keep the promise] unless he is concerned with the interests and goods these define, in short with the well-being of the person with whom he has joined some segment of his own life." Melden is also able to use this rights framework to explain the guilt we feel at breaking a promise, and to provide some of the excusing conditions which justify one in breaking a promise. His arguments are unique in the sense that he argues—against Rawls and others—that the unique characteristics of individuals are important rather than irrelevant in determining how we should treat others. As Melden says, "Human beings do not come out of the same mold, with the same interests and the same goods that play the same role in the same plans and projects."

As a result of the work of Melden and Brandt, philosophers are debating the issues of utilitarianism vs. a deontological theory of rights with new vigor and at greater levels of sophistication. Thanks in part to the efforts of the four authors included here, philosophical ethics has not died, but is one of the more exciting areas of contemporary philosophy.

VALUE-JUDGMENTS:
THEIR IMPLICIT GENERALITY

Charles L. Stevenson

1

Let me indicate briefly what I plan to do in my paper. I shall first summarize a meta-evaluative theory that I worked out some years ago. It is sometimes called an "emotive" theory, and is meta-evaluative in that it aims not at making value-judgments but rather at analyzing their meaning and at characterizing the reasons that can be given in support of them. After summarizing the theory I shall go on to test it, with attention to some points that I have previously neglected. In particular, I shall consider whether it can account for our tendency, in every-day discussions, to reject self-excepting judgments—judgments in which a man absolves himself from rules that he would have others obey. And I shall discuss, more broadly, our inclination to ascribe an implicit generality to our judgments—an inclination that is in accord with what Richard Hare has called "the thesis of universalizability." An explanation of such matters may at first seem to lie well beyond an emotive theory, as if showing that the theory can become tenable only if an important restriction is *superimposed* upon it. I shall argue, on the contrary, that the explanation can be developed in a manner that lies comfortably *within* an emotive theory.

2

I shall venture to summarize an emotive theory (partially, to be sure) by making the following five statements:

(1) A value-judgment about x typically expresses the speaker's attitude (of favor or disfavor, approval or disapproval, etc.) to x. It expresses rather than describes that attitude, so it must be distinguished from an introspective remark that merely expresses the speaker's *belief about* his attitude.

(2) A value-judgment also enables a speaker to *invite* any hearer or hearers to share his attitude—though "invite" is some-

times too weak a term and needs to be replaced by "urge." It is this inviting or urging factor that enables the speaker to have a potential influence, though a very small one, in preserving or changing the customs (the "mores," as Sumner called them) of his society.

(3) Both of the above functions, which lead us to speak of value-judgments as laudatory or derogatory, and which fit them for use in commending, praising, disparaging, reprimanding, and so on, become possible because the value-terms have an emotive meaning, which is akin to what J. L. Austin called a special "illocutionary force." That aspect of their meaning or force is over and above any factual information that the terms are used to convey or suggest.

(4) But value-judgments can be supported by factual reasons. The reasons, concerned with the nature and consequences of what is judged, are reasons *for approving or disapproving.* Suppose, for instance, that Mr. A approves of x, claiming that it is right, whereas Mr. B initially disapproves of x, claiming that it is wrong. Perhaps Mr. A can then give Mr. B reasons for approving of x—reasons that disclose consequences of x that Mr. B didn't previously know about, consequences which Mr. B is inclined to approve. These reasons may change Mr. B's attitude to x, leading him to approve of it, and to agree with Mr. A in saying that x is right. The agreement will be "in attitude."

(5) To what extent could reasons for approving or disapproving, if fully used, lead people to agree (in attitude) on evaluative matters? To ask that is to ask about the extent to which individual differences in people's attitudes would cease to exist in the light of full factual information. The answer is uncertain insofar as it bears on all cases; but in many cases one can hope, at least, that a reasoned solution of evaluative disagreements will be possible.

3

As I have remarked, I want to *test* the theory that I have summarized, asking whether it can give an acceptable account of certain convictions that we are likely, in our every-day discussions of values, to take for granted. These same convictions have not escaped theoretical attention, so let me introduce them with references to the history of philosophy.

Samuel Clarke, in 1705, propounded what he called "the rule of equity"—a rule reminiscent of the Golden Rule:

> Whatever I judge reasonable or unreasonable that another should do for me, that by the same judgment I declare reasonable or unreasonable that I should *in the like case* do for him.

Clarke considered his rule to be true a priori; and whatever we may think of its a priori status we shall not be inclined, I trust, to deny its plausibility.

There are various differences, to be sure, between Clarke's rule of equity and the categorical imperative that was stated several generations later by Immanuel Kant; but it is not too much to say that Clarke's view partially anticipated Kant's. Rather than go into the complexities of Kant's work, however, let me turn to a view developed several generations still later by Henry Sidgwick, whose *Methods of Ethics* was first published in 1874.

Sidgwick, after making favorable comments about Clarke's rule of equity, stated a principle that closely neighbored it:

> If I judge any action to be right for myself, I implicitly judge it to be right for any other person whose nature and circumstances do not differ from mine in certain important respects.

The words, "in certain important respects," raise a question: just who is estimating the *importance* of the respects? Sidgwick doesn't quite tell us, but I shall assume that his principle is to be interpreted as if the following words were added to it: "—that is to say, in respects that I myself would claim or acknowledge to be important in deciding whether such an act is right." The words "I myself," of course, will continue to refer to whatever speaker it is who is applying the principle to his judgments.

The principle, so interpreted, is so much in accord with our everyday convictions that I shall take it as my point of departure. To clarify it let me mention a judgment that violates it—an absurd judgment, to be sure, but one that becomes of interest because the principle proclaims it as absurd. Consider, then, the judgment,

> It is right for me to steal but not right for others to steal—that being so no matter how closely the nature and circumstances of the others resemble mine.

Such a judgment can be called "exclusively self-excepting." Any speaker, if he were to make the judgment, would be maintaining that It is not right to steal applies to every person save one, that person being the speaker himself; and he would be singling himself out merely by using indexical pronouns ("me" and "mine"), and hence he would be acknowledging that the properties that describe him, concerned with his nature and circumstances, would provide no impersonal grounds for the special status that he was claiming for himself. The example, though not in Sidgwick, will serve to typify the many parallel judgments, all of them exclusively self-excepting, that Sidgwick's principle declares to be untenable.

We must be careful not to confuse an exclusively self-excepting judgment with one of a quite different sort—a judgment in which a speaker claims that something is right for him under his circumstances while acknowledging that it is wrong under most circumstances. A man who steals to prevent his children from starving, for instance, may say, "Although stealing is wrong under most circumstances, it is right for me to steal, and right for anyone else to steal if his children, too, are starving." Such a judgment, by the last part of it, claims no privilege that he refuses to grant to others whose circumstances resemble his. So although it is a self-favoring judgment, it is not exclusively self-excepting, and it does not, of course, violate Sidgwick's principle.

I am not suggesting that Sidgwick would therefore have accepted the man's judgment about stealing. I want merely to say that in deciding whether to accept or reject it he would have been guided by reflections that lie beyond his principle. He himself said that the principle "manifestly does not give full guidance," implying that a judgment must be rejected if it violates the principle, but may also be rejected, on other grounds, even if it conforms to the principle.

It is because of Sidgwick's modest claim for his principle that I have interpreted his words, "in certain important respects," to refer to the speaker's own claim about importance. Thus when a speaker says, "It is right for me to steal, and right for anyone else to steal if his children, too, are starving," he is generalizing about circumstances that *he* claims, implicitly, to be important. Anyone else, including Sidgwick, is privileged to disagree with that claim, but must acknowledge that the speaker has complied with the principle. The disagreement would lie beyond the principle.

Having introduced Sidgwick's principle I must go on to see whether or not an emotive theory can explain why it gives us the strong impression, at least, of being axiomatically true. I shall find it convenient to deal mainly with judgments that violate the principle—exclusively self-excepting judgments of the sort that I mentioned well above. By attempting to explain why they are commonly rejected I shall be attempting, by implication, to explain why the principle is commonly accepted.

4

Let me first point out—as I can do, surely, without misdescribing human nature—that some people are appropriately said to be altruistic, and are also said to be kind, considerate, benevolent, socially dedicated, and so on. They not only desire the welfare of others but in good measure desire it for its own sake. They may believe that the welfare of others is often a means to their own welfare; but even when they find that that is not the case—even when they find that the welfare of others can be obtained only at a considerable sacrifice of their own—their desire for the welfare of others continues to predominate.

Now such people, obviously enough, are unlikely to have *attitudes* that are self-excepting. And for them an acceptance of Sidgwick's principle is easily explained. By an emotive theory their judgments express their attitudes. If they made exclusively self-excepting judgments, then, they would be expressing exclusively self-excepting attitudes. And they will make no such judgments so long as they have no such attitudes.

I am speaking, of course, of a high degree of altruism that is characteristic of *some* people. Should I say, more cautiously, that it is characteristic of some people to some extent, and on some occasions? However that may be, it will not do to take altruism as somehow foreign to human nature. It provides a vectorial force that serves, whenever present, to lead people to conform to Sidgwick's principle—though for psychological reasons, to be sure, rather than for reasons that are synthetic a priori.

There can be no thought, however, of claiming that altruism is sufficiently prevalent to account for the *virtually universal* acceptance, in common life, of Sidgwick's principle. There are people who do indeed have exclusively self-excepting *attitudes*, as is evident from their actions. Even so, they do not express those attitudes (apart from pretences that they are *not* exclusively self-excepting) by using such terms as "right" and "wrong"; they do not express them by exclusively self-excepting *judgments*. I must now explain why that is so; and my aim will be to show that the explanation can continue to be developed from an emotive theory, so long as that theory is not separated, artificially, from its psychological background.

5

I can best begin my explanation by pointing out that people often have occasion to hold back their judgments—to hold them back in the sense of leaving them unuttered. That is true even when their corresponding attitudes are of an every-day sort, having nothing to do with self-exception. A Democrat, for instance, when a guest at dinner of a man who is known to be an uncompromising Republican, may refrain from making judgments (aloud) that favor the Democratic party—not because he is without a partial inclination to make them, but simply because, under the circumstances, he feels that he must hold them back to avoid offending his host, or to avoid provoking a heated discussion that he considers untimely. Or again, it may happen that a father, however much he may want his son to become a lawyer, will avoid telling his son that he ought to go to law school, simply because he thinks that his son, being in a mood of rebellion from parental authority, will be particularly averse to going to law school if his father connects that with an "ought." There are innumerable cases in which judgments are held back, and for reasons that may differ from those that I have mentioned—reasons that bear on modesty, for instance, or on fear.

We shall better understand the occasions for holding judgments back if we bear in mind that the judgments, if uttered, would typically do *more* than express the speaker's attitudes. They would also invite others to share those attitudes. (See the second of my remarks, in Section 2, about the emotive theory, remembering that I use "invite" to do service, not infrequently, for a stronger term, such as "urge".) Now invitations of that sort, attending expressions of attitude, can under certain circumstances have effects that a speaker does not welcome, as the above examples have illustrated. A speaker holds back his judgments, accordingly, when he anticipates those effects and has a predominating desire to avoid them.

Ordinarily, a man will hold back his judgments because of their special content, or because of the particular people to whom he is speaking. The Democrat of my example may hold back his pro-Democratic judgments when talking to his Republican host, but may have no occasion to hold back various other judgments from his host; and he may have no occasion to hold back his pro-Democratic judgments when talking to people elsewhere. So it is, *mutatis mutandis*, for many other examples.

But I have been speaking about "everyday" judgments, and must now return to judgments that are exclusively self-excepting. I shall attempt to show that my remarks have a straightforward bearing on the latter judgments. I shall claim that a man, in avoiding (as is typical) even the suspicion of making such judgments, will be doing so because he has strong reasons for holding the judgments back—that being true no matter how deeply rooted his self-excepting *attitudes* may be. Nor is the man likely to be insensitive to those reasons. For unlike the reasons that lead "everyday" judgments to be held back, which arise (as I have just remarked) only in special cases, the reasons that lead exclusively self-excepting judgments to be held back are of a sort that arise in virtually all cases.

But just what are those reasons? And why do they apply so strongly and so ubiquitously to judgments that are exclusively self-excepting? In essentials, my answer is very simple, and runs as follows.

When a man has an exclusively self-excepting *attitude* he is favoring, as we have seen, some privilege or exemption that he reserves just for himself, without wanting to extend it to others, no matter how much their nature and circumstances resemble his. But human nature being what it is, he can have no real hope of getting others to share that attitude, and indeed, little hope of getting others to countenance it. It is one thing for him to have a strongly self-centered attitude, and quite another thing for him to expect others to have a strongly *him*-centered attitude. So if he were to express his attitude by a judgment, thereby inviting others to share it, he would be issuing an invitation virtually destined to be rejected, and rejected, normally, with indignation. Now an invitation virtually destined to be so rejected would not serve its purpose. The speaker would have nothing to gain by it and perhaps something to lose by it. Realizing that, a speaker who is at first inclined to make such a judgment will not in fact make it. He will leave it unuttered.

In saying that I am not calling Sidgwick's principle into question. I am being faithful to it, though "in my fashion." I am, however, criticizing the grounds that Sidgwick gave for it. He thought that it had to be established by an appeal to synthetic a priori knowledge. I am replacing that appeal, consonantly with an emotive theory, by an appeal to empirical psychology.

Let me emphasize, at the expense of partial repetition, the sort of psychology to which I am appealing—a very simple psychology that can be tested in daily life.

The three remarks that follow deserve special attention. (1) Our attitudes strongly tend toward generality: they tend to be directed to all objects (all things, actions, people, and so forth) of this or that sort, and tend to be directed to a given object only because it is found to be of that sort. (2) But that tendency can be offset, and it is particularly likely to be offset by a man's self-interest. Thus when Mr. X favors himself more than others, and without taking account of the sort of man he is, his attitude has a generality that is offset by an exception: his attitude becomes exclusively self-excepting. (3) Other people, however, will not have attitudes (save in rare cases) whose generality is offset by an exclusive partiality to Mr. X. Their attitudes may sometimes depart from generality in favor of themselves, but not in favor of him. From their point of view an exclusive exception in favor of him would be dismissed as arbitrary.

My three remarks prepare the way for this conclusion: when a man claims a special privilege for himself, other people will grant it to him only if they consider him the sort of man to whom, in general, they want to grant the privilege. I need only add, then, that a man soon becomes aware of that, and makes his judgments accordingly. He may continue to have exclusively self-excepting attitudes, but he will realize that if he were to make corresponding judgments, inviting others to share those attitudes, he would be issuing pointless invitations. So he holds back those judgments, and restricts himself, in accordance with

Sidgwick's principle, to judgments that have a chance, at least, of serving their purpose.

Are my remarks vulnerable? They must surely be taken into serious consideration; and if, like so many psychological generalizations, they are in need of qualifications, the qualifications are not likely, I trust, to undermine my explanation of why Sidgwick's principle is so widely accepted.

Let me illustrate what I am saying by an example. A certain Mr. Smith, during a winter when fuel is in short supply, says that it is wrong for others to heat their houses to high temperatures, but is not apologetic for the high temperature of his own house. We ask him, in surprise, how his case differs from that of others, and in politeness suggest an "out" for him, saying, "Perhaps your special circumstances—concerned, say, with the state of your health—provide you with a justification that others do not have." But Smith rejects the "out," and with a certain bravado (so I shall artificially assume) tells us that there is no difference between his case and theirs that is worth mentioning. "I am nevertheless maintaining," he says, "that the fuel shortage makes it wrong for *others* to heat their houses to high temperatures, but doesn't make it wrong for *me* to do it." Now if he takes that stand we shall unhesitatingly reply, and in no uncertain terms, that we don't intend to let him get away with his judgment. "How can you expect us," we shall say, "arbitrarily to single just you out in that fashion—just you rather than any other person we might mention? You speak of a responsibility that you too could bear, and talk as if we ought to let you push it off on other people's shoulders (including our own shoulders)." We shall thereby be letting Smith know, as he has somehow managed not to know, that our attitudes are not going to be arbitrarily centered on Smith; we shall be letting him know that the invitation attending his judgment is one that we indignantly reject. And Smith, realizing that our remarks typify the social pressure to which he will be subjected, will see that his judgment is pointless, and will not persist in making it.

Such, though only in essentials, is my explanation of why Sidgwick's principle is not violated—an explanation that is not in need, as I see it, of being supplemented by an appeal to synthetic a priori knowledge. A man may accept the principle because he is strongly altruistic; but even when he lacks altruism he will still accept the principle, realizing that a violation of it wouldn't get him anywhere.

Let me add that my explanation is of a sort that might be called "rationale-disclosing." People are often poorly aware of the forces that guide their judgments, having no more than half-felt promptings about them, and promptings that are well mingled with habits that they form in imitating others. The purpose of a rationale-disclosing explanation is to transform those half-felt promptings into articulate beliefs.

6

I have so far been dealing only with interpersonal situations—situations in which a man is engaged in a discussion with other people, and makes or holds back a judgment with attention to its potential effects on *them*. I must go on, supplementing my explanation, to deal with less typical but interesting situations that are not interpersonal.

I have in mind the judgments that a man confides to his diary, taking precautions to let no one read it but himself. Diaries of that sort, in spite of the diarist's precautions, have often yielded their secrets to biographers, and have shown that exclusively self-excepting judgments are absent even from them. I must explain that, since it seems to stand apart from what I have previously said. The diarist is making judgments that he believes to be secret; and the invitations that attend them will be in abeyance, as if issued by his present self to his later self only. He feels, then, that he is in a position to disregard any social pressure that would otherwise lead him to hold back his judgments, including his exclusively self-excepting judgments. Even so, he avoids the latter judgments. Why is that the case?

My answer is again a simple one, and to this effect: the pointlessness of self-excepting judgments is so pervasive that it deprives them of *any* sort of motivation, in a diary or elsewhere. To justify that answer I shall first call attention to judgments that are *not* exclusively self-excepting, with attention to the motives that lead *them* to be *included* in a diary; and I shall argue that no such motives arise for judgments that are exclusively self-excepting.

For an example of judgments that are not exclusively self-excepting let me consider a man whose attitude to a dictator, under whom he lives, is entirely hostile. He is afraid, in his conversations with others, to make correspondingly hostile judgments; but in his diary (carefully hidden) he writes down many such judgments, and many reasons in support of them. What motives is he likely to have?

Quite possibly, he is looking ahead to a time when he *can* address his judgments to others. Perhaps an underground movement will arise, or perhaps he can get away to another country. He can then repeat his judgments under circumstances that give them a chance of being influential. Meanwhile his diary is in the nature of a rehearsal—a rehearsal for a role that he hopes to play later in the presence of an audience.

Such a man has indeed a motive for including judgments in his diary. We have quite a different situation, however, when we turn to another sort of man, whose attitudes are exclusively self-excepting. He will not have the motive in question. If he so much as thought of troubling his diary with judgments corresponding to *those* attitudes he would realize that as a rehearsal they would be in vain. As we have previously seen, no audience, at any time or at any place, would put up with the exclusively self-excepting role for which he was rehearsing.

But let me say something more about the diarist who opposes the dictator. His judgments may arise from a further motive, and a very strong one. He may be intent on fixing his adverse attitude, along with the reasons that support it, firmly in his mind, so that he will not be talked out of it by censored news reports, and will not become half-a-man (as he may put it) by yielding to his unreflective moods, or by resigning himself to apathy. His secret judgments will then be akin to *resolutions*. They will be made not only with attention to his possible influence on others (subsequently or elsewhere) but also with attention to what he feels to be the integrity of his own personality.

What shall be said of that motive? Could it, *mutatis mutandis*, lead a man to fix in his mind various attitudes that are arbitrarily self-excepting? That is not, I suspect, impossible. The man would be the very opposite of a man who is socially dedicated: he would be trying to resist a temptation, as it were, to respect the needs of others. And yet such a man can perhaps be found, and not necessarily in a prison. But he too will be unlikely, even in a diary, to make *judgments* that are exclusively self-excepting. He might, avoiding the terms "right" and "wrong," write down something like this: "I must resist those who are trying to hinder me; I must continue to take advantage of them without letting them take advantage of me." But he would be uncomfortable in saying, "Regardless of circumstances, various things are right

when I do them and wrong when others do them." For in bol-
stering up his exclusively self-excepting attitudes he will be com-
batting a social pressure whose force he has felt since childhood.
He will not find that easy, and he will find it harder if he does it
by depending on the words "right" and "wrong." Those words
would bring memories of the very different purposes for which
others have used them in interpersonal situations. They might
lead him to see himself as others see him. And that he must
avoid, else his temptation to altruism might win out in conflict
with his self-centered attitudes. It is only the latter attitude that
he is trying to encourage in himself.

Of the two motives that I have mentioned, concerned respectively with rehearsals and with resolutions, the first one, for exclusively self-excepting judgments, wholly drops out, and the
second one strongly tends to drop out. And that does much to
account for the fact that a man will let his judgments—even in a
diary, and even if his attitudes are self-excepting—conform to
Sidgwick's principle. A lack of motivation filters out the judgments (the judgments, not the attitudes) that stand in opposition to the principle, leaving the principle itself unquestioned.

I should properly say more in this connection, to make sure
that other motives, if they exist, can be handled in a parallel
way. I have said enough, however, to suggest that the "privacy"
of a man's diary cannot put him outside of his society. If his
judgments are not addressed to actual readers they are nevertheless written down in the presence of imagined readers; and
those imagined readers can continue to exert an influence on
what he writes.

7

In the remainder of my paper I shall return to interpersonal
situations, which will be sufficient to illustrate the points that I
shall be defending. But I shall no longer limit my attention to
judgments that are *self*-excepting. I shall deal with a larger class
of judgments: namely those that introduce exclusive exceptions
of any sort. I shall discuss a broad principle that stands opposed
to all such judgments.

The latter principle, too, has had its varied history, but has
taken on a special interest in the past two or three decades. It
has been defended at length by Marcus Singer and by Richard
Hare, and has occasioned helpful comments by E. A. Gellner.

In my own discussion of the principle I shall be concerned only with present-day versions of it, staying rather close to the version that Hare has called the "thesis of universalizability." I shall restate and discuss the principle in my own way, and shall rebaptize it as the "principle of implicit generality"; but those acquainted with Hare's work will readily see, I trust, that when I diverge from him—implying that he leaves the principle imperfectly connected with the rest of his view and is therefore in danger of making too much of it—my divergence will not be unattended by an indebtedness to him.

To introduce the principle I must distinguish, following Gellner but without using his terminology, between singularizing and nonsingularizing properties. I shall say that a property is singularizing just in case it can be designated only with the help of a singular term—only with the help of a proper name, or a surrogate of a proper name. Among the surrogates I shall include indexical expressions and also definite descriptions when their identifying function takes precedence over their describing function. Thus the property of *being John's friend* is singularizing (because of the proper name, "John's"); and so is the property of *being my friend* (since "my" is indexical); and so is the property of *being a friend of the first surgeon* who transplanted a heart (because "the first surgeon . . ." introduces a definite description). But the property of *having many friends* (which uses neither a proper name nor a surrogate of it) is nonsingularizing.

It will be convenient to extend the distinction, letting it apply to generalizations as well as to properties. A generalization will be singularizing if it makes *any* nonvacuous reference to a singularizing property; otherwise it will be nonsingularizing.

Given the distinction I can lead up to the principle by the following example:

> When a man says, "Jones's act was praiseworthy," he is thereby committed to this further assertion: "There is some [perhaps highly complex] factual property, P, which satisfies the following conditions:
> (1) P is nonsingularizing, and
> (2) Jones's act had P, and
> (3) Every act that has P is praiseworthy."

I shall discuss condition (1), with its reference to a nonsingularizing property, in just a moment. Meanwhile let me point out that the principle is concerned with implicit generality (or universalizability) because of condition (3). The speaker's initial judgment, being explicitly just about Jones's act, may seem to have no connection with a generalization; but according to the principle it commits him to the generalization that (3) introduces. It should be particularly noted, however, that the subject term of (3) does not refer to a property by naming it or otherwise fully identifying it; it refers only to *some* factual property that satisfies conditions (1) and (2). There will be many properties of that sort. There will also be many corresponding generalizations, each naming or otherwise fully identifying such a property by its subject term. So the speaker is committed, according to the principle, only to one or another of that *set* of generalizations. If he goes on to mention one of them as the one that he accepts—thereby going beyond his commitment, though in a way that he may find essential in introducing further discussion—he will have a choice, within broad limits, of just what his generalization (with a fully identified property mentioned by its subject term) will be.

My selected example readily suggests others that resemble it. The term "praiseworthy" can be replaced throughout by "virtuous," or "reprehensible," or "right," or "wrong," and so on. There are further cases in which the initial judgment about an act can be replaced by one about a person, for instance, and in such a way as this:

> When a man says, "Jane ought to be pensioned," he is committed to this further assertion: "Jane has some factual and nonsingularizing property, P, such that anyone who has P ought to be pensioned."

And there are cases in which it is necessary, to insure a commitment to a generalization that is nonsingularizing, to introduce more than one bound property-variable, as in

> When a man says, "Many people have cars that are better than mine," he is committed to this further assertion: "There are factual and nonsingularizing properties, P and Q, such that my car has P and many people's cars have Q, and such that any car having Q is better than a car having P."

Or again,

> When a man says, "John ought to marry Mary," he is com-
> mitted to this further assertion: "There are factual and non-
> singularizing properties, P, Q, and R, such that John has P
> and Mary has Q and John has R to Mary, and such that if
> any man has P and stands in relation R to a woman who
> has Q, then that man ought to marry that woman."

The principle deals with what is common to the examples. In
each example there is an initial judgment that is *not* explicitly
general and nonsingularizing. And anyone who makes such a
judgment, according to the principle, is committed to a judgment that *is* explicitly general and nonsingularizing, together
with the claim that his initial judgment is a special case of it.

In so stating the principle let me make clear, with deliberate
repetition, that when I speak of a generalization I am not in-
sisting that its subject term must designate a property that is
named or otherwise fully identified. The generalization must be
an "all" generalization or the equivalent of that; but its subject
term may include one or more variables that are bound by the
word "some." A man will usually have occasion to go beyond
his commitment, identifying the subject term of his generalization more fully; but as I have previously remarked, the principle
allows him a choice, within broad limits, of how he will proceed
to do so.

Let me now explain why the principle is restricted (in Hare's
manner) to nonsingularizing properties, and hence to nonsingularizing generalizations. The purpose of the restriction is to
give the principle a needed strength without undermining its
immediately felt plausibility. Whether it adequately serves that
purpose has occasionally been questioned; but there can be no
doubt that the restriction takes a large step in the right direction, and to that extent, at least, I shall attempt to defend it. Let
me return in that connection to the second of the above examples.

Suppose that a certain speaker, having initially made the
judgment, "Jane ought to be pensioned," goes on to say, "Jane is
a child of Sam Robinson, and every child of his ought to be pensioned." Since the speaker's remarks *include* a generalization it
may seem superfluous for us to remind him that he is *committed*
to a generalization. But the reminder would not be inap-

propriate. We shall be inclined to feel that his initial judgment brings with it a stronger commitment than any that he has as yet shown signs of acknowledging—a commitment to a non-singularizing generalization rather than to one (like his) that is singularizing. He has simply gone from a privilege that he claims for Jane to a privilege that he claims for her father's children, and we shall expect a further generalization, bearing on the latter claim. Realizing that, the speaker may go on, for instance, to say: "Jane is the child of a man who was disabled while fighting for his country; and children of all such men ought to be pensioned." Only then, we shall be inclined to feel, will the speaker be taking account of his "real" commitment. We may or may not, of course, agree with the latter generalization; nor will the speaker's initial judgment require him to make just that generalization. But we shall be inclined to feel that the speaker is committed to some or another generalization that is non-singularizing, and that any principle requiring less than that would be unnecessarily weak. I speak only of what we are inclined to feel; but on this matter our inclination cannot easily be dismissed.

Let me immediately add, however, that my remarks raise a question. Suppose, in the above example, that the speaker and Jane and her father are all citizens of the United States; and suppose that the speaker, so far as Jane's pension is concerned, disclaims any interest in a nonsingularizing generalization insofar as it bears on countries other than the United States. "I want to limit my generalization," he says, "to citizens of my own country, having no advice to give about citizens of other countries." Will we be inclined to feel that he is violating his commitment? We may have doubts about that, along with doubts as to whether the principle of implicit generality, as I have stated it, can be accepted without qualification. But that is a matter that I shall discuss later. Meanwhile I shall assume, though perhaps temporarily, that the doubts can be dispelled.

So much, then, for my *statement* of the principle. Let me now go on to make some further remarks about it. In particular, I want to transfer my rationale-disclosing remarks about Sidgwick's principle to the present, broader principle.

8

An exclusively self-excepting judgment, when phrased in the terminology of the principle of implicit generality rather than in the terminology of Sidgwick's principle, can be exemplified in this way:

> It is right for me to do it, even though I have *no* factual and nonsingularizing property, P, such that it would be right for anyone who has P to do it.

There is no longer a Sidgwick-like reference to the speaker's nature and circumstances; but note that the variable, "P," can range over properties that describe them, and that the terms, "nature" and "circumstances," are extremely broad—so broad that they would do little more, if retained, than confirm the appropriateness of a description that refers to factual and non-singularizing properties. So without denying minor differences, I shall assume that Sidgwick's principle and the principle of implicit generality, with regard to self-excepting judgments, have implications that are essentially alike; and I shall assume that the latter principle, in standing opposed to those judgments, lends itself to the same rationale-disclosing explanation (to the effect that the judgments would be pointless) that I have given for Sidgwick's principle.

But the principle of implicit generality applies to many other examples, to which my previous remarks have still to be transferred. The simplest examples are those in which a judgment is made of *things*, and under circumstances where the speaker's attitudes are themselves implicitly general—i.e., directed to all members of a *class* of things, the class being defined by a property that is factual and nonsingularizing. Any person is likely to have such an attitude to typewriters, for instance; so when he says, "That typewriter is a good one" he will have no hesitation in accepting his commitment, which will run, "That typewriter has some factual and nonsingularizing property, P, such that every typewriter having P is a good one." He is generalizing his initial judgment in a way that simply mirrors the generality of his attitude.

My remark remains close to one that I made previously (Section 5), where I said that a man might accept Sidgwick's principle because, being highly altruistic, he has an attitude whose tendency to generality is not offset by self-interest. My example about typewriters may seem to resist a comparison to an example about altruism; but the two are alike in showing that an attitude, when general, readily leads to a general judgment.

I should properly consider a great number of other judgments, but shall pause to mention only two of them. Both are "exclusively *group*-excepting," and both are of a sort to which the principle of implicit generality stands opposed.

Consider the judgment:

> The citizens of Fairhaven ought to be exempted from taxes, even though they have *no* factual and singularizing property, P, such that everyone having P ought to be exempted from taxes.

The judgment, I trust, is one that no one will make, and perhaps because no one will have a predominating attitude that prompts it. But let me assume that a certain man has such an attitude, arising from an exclusive loyalty to his friends in Fairhaven—exclusive in the sense that he does not want others to have such a loyalty, regardless of conditions, to the citizens of any other town. Even so, he will not bother to make the corresponding judgment, which could serve its purpose—that of helping to secure the exemption in question—only if its accompanying invitation had a chance of being accepted both inside and outside of Fairhaven. But outside of Fairhaven, in particular, it would only provoke the indignant question, "How can you expect us to be arbitrary in selecting just *that* group of people for the privilege?" The judgment would be pointless, and held back for that reason.

The psychological principles underlying the rejection of the judgment are very close to those that I have previously mentioned (Section 5). For (1) attitudes tend toward a *nonsingularizing* generality with respect to their objects; but (2) that tendency can be offset not only by self-interest but also by a less usual force that arises from an *exclusive* loyalty to a *group*. Moreover, (3) *any* offsetting force is likely to take a different direction for different people. So if a person were to invite others to share the exclusively group-excepting attitude in question he would find few people, and too few for his purpose, who would share it with just *his* departures from generality. Realizing that, no person, after a moment's reflection, would waste his time in making a judgment that issues such an invitation.

Let me now turn to a neighboring example that deals with an "exclusively nation-excepting" judgment. It is of interest because it raises a question—like the last part of my example about Jane's pension—as to whether my statement of the principle of implicit generality requires a qualification.

Suppose that the leader of nation N, like a present-day Alexander or a present-day Napoleon, makes the claim:

Nation N ought to enlarge its boundaries by conquest.

He will get nowhere with his judgment, of course, if he addresses it to nations who are in immediate danger of being conquered; and he will not get very far with it if he addresses it to the remaining nations, who are likely to fear that they may be next. He has a chance, however, of getting somewhere by addressing it to the people in his own nation. And in so addressing it he may be half-inclined to add the commitment-rejecting judgment:

It is not the case that nation N has some factual and non-singularizing property, P, such that any nation having P ought to enlarge its boundaries by conquest.

If he does add this commitment-rejecting judgment he will be appealing, by his initial judgment, only to his people's national self-interest. Will he be content to do that?

I think not, and for this reason: his commitment requires so little of him that he will see no advantage in rejecting it. The people of nation N, being human, will be likely to have certain aspirations that lie beyond their national self-interest: they may want, for instance, to have others adopt their religion (or irreligion), or to have others adopt their form of government; or they may want to make the people of their race, throughout the world, predominate over people of other races; or they may want to develop a world state that they think will serve, after initial wars are ended, to preserve peace. The leader of N will need to appeal to those aspirations. He will be in a position to accept his commitment by claiming that *any* nation having *those* aspirations ought to enlarge its boundaries by conquest.

But will he not (it may be asked) want to discourage conquests by other nations, even though they too have those aspirations? Yes, usually; but how can he use value-judgments to do so? Other nations, initially fearing his conquests, would have redoubled fears if they found that he was reserving the right of conquest to N, denying it to them. If so minded (as to be sure they might not be), and if sufficiently powerful, they would take steps toward conquest without being in the least deterred by evaluative remonstrances from a nation like N—remonstrances that they would interpret as a way of urging them to let N dominate them. The leader of N, then, will have nothing to lose by accepting the commitment that attends his pro-aggressive judgment, which requires no more than that he generalize his judgment in *some* nonsingularizing way. And he will have something to gain by selecting a nonsingularizing generalization that reminds his own people of aspirations that lie beyond their national self-interest. If he appealed *only* to their national self-interest he would be neglecting an appeal to aspirations that could *reinforce* their national self-interest, and would thus be neglecting a means of strengthening their support for his policy.

Let me acknowledge, however, that a full exploration of such examples would require a more careful study than I can here develop. It might disclose cases in which the principle of implicit generality, as I have stated it, would no longer bring with it the immediate, unquestioning acceptance that I am inclined to claim for it. *If* so, and *if* the principle is to insure its acceptance, then my statement of it will need a weakening qualification—a qualification to the effect that a nonsingularizing generalization, to which a speaker is normally committed, can sometimes give place to a singularizing generalization, though only when the latter bears on so large a group of people that the speaker is content to address it solely to them, abandoning any thought of defending it to people outside the group.

I doubt, let me repeat, that the leader of N would want to resort to such a generalization; but if he did he could introduce and state it in some such way as this:

> By enlarging its boundaries by conquest N would be taking a step essential to its own welfare; and nation N ought to take all such steps, no matter what effect they may have on the welfare of other nations.

The qualified principle would permit him, within N, to repudiate any supplementary, nonsingularizing generalization. But those in N who opposed his claim would not, it must be remembered, be left without arguments. Instead of opposing him on the ground that he was violating the (qualified) principle, they could do so on grounds that lie beyond the principle. For the principle, whether qualified or not, is like Sidgwick's in that it "manifestly does not give full guidance."

9

My remarks are sufficient, I trust, to show that the principle of implicit generality can be accounted for without being taken as a priori and synthetic. Let me now ask whether it can plausibly be taken, consonantly with a slightly amended emotive theory, as a priori and analytic. Is the principle implied by the very meaning of value-judgments?

As I see it, the question can be answered by a flip of a coin. Our evaluative language is open to reconstruction: it leaves us with a choice of building an implicit generality into it, making the principle analytically a priori, or of building an implicit generality out of it, leaving the principle without an a priori status. And for either way of making the choice (apart from considerations of grammatical simplicity) the result of it will have no implications that are of practical interest. Let me explain further.

If the principle is to be built into our language it will require two senses of such a term as "right." "Right-I" will have only the expressing and inviting functions that I have mentioned, and will be restricted to contexts that are explicitly general and non-singularizing. "Right-II" will have a sense restricted to other contexts, and for the simplest of those contexts will be definable with the help of "right-I" in the following manner:

x is right-II $=$df.   x has some factual and nonsingularizing property, P, such that anything having P is right-I.

Once the distinction between right-I and right-II has been introduced, the Roman numerals can be dropped, being redundant in their normal contexts. So when a man says of a certain x that it is right, and we remind him of his commitment, we shall simply be reminding him of what is analytically contained in his judgment.

For more complicated contexts, and for terms other than "right," the principle of implicit generality can be built into our language in a parallel way. The more complicated contexts will include, of course, those that introduce more than one property-variable, as illustrated in Section 7. Moreover, *if* the principle retains its plausibility only when subject to a weakening qualification—about which I have expressed an uncertainty rather than a conviction—then that qualification too can be built into our language.

An emotive theory in no way loses its identity by such a procedure, for an acceptance of it makes the theory neither weaker nor stronger. The procedure simply gives a linguistic turn to a rule that arises from people's *purposes* in judging—a rule that they will follow whether they consider it linguistic or not. As we have seen, the principle of implicit generality has its psychological sanctions: violations of it are easily seen to be pointless. Any further sanction of it, though gratuitous, will not be foreign to it. So if a further sanction is sought in a definitional rule there will be no practical gain or loss. In the *half*-formalized language of everyday life, however, the definitional rule is not already "there" in the way that a definitional rule is "there" in a logical or mathematical calculus; and since, if introduced, it will merely represent an effort to deter people from saying what in any case they do not want to say, it will place no new constraint on the things that people do want to say.

Similar remarks by no means apply to many other definitional rules that are likely to be encountered in value-theory. Consider, for instance, what happens when the laudatory terms, remaining laudatory, are defined to mean, in part, *conducive to the greatest happiness of the greatest number*. The rule then tends to preempt the laudatory terms for Utilitarians, leaving others with no convenient terms for expressing an opposing view. Though phrased as a definition it is tantamount to a value-judgment, and no less subject to rejection than when the value-judgment is otherwise expressed. Every caution is needed, accordingly, in preventing all such definitions from entering into a *meta*-evaluative analysis, where their evaluative import would be disguised. Nor will a Utilitarian be content with that disguise when he realizes that the same disguise, and for a decidedly different purpose, is embodied in the "newspeak" of Orwell's novel, where the laudatory terms are defined to mean, in part, *in accordance with the will of Big Brother*. An emotive theory, instead of rebuilding our language with definitions of that kind, must simply explain what is at issue when others attempt to do so.

When the principle of implicit generality is in question, however, that sort of issue does not arise. If the principle is built into our language—as is meta-evaluatively defensible but not mandatory—the value terms are not preempted for a special use.

They are left with all the uses that anyone, regardless of his evaluative position, will want to preserve for them. That is a consequence of the view that I have been defending. An emotive analysis, together with its psychological background, implies that *any* speaker will easily recognize a violation of the principle as pointless.

I have gone into similar matters in chapter IX of my *Ethics and Language*, where I dealt with definitions that are persuasive in tendency, and also in the first section of chapter X, where I explained the conditions under which the evaluative terms can be assigned a cognitive meaning *without* being persuasive in tendency.

Let me pause to indicate, though all too briefly, the extent to which I diverge from Richard Hare. He considers his prescriptivism (a near-emotivism) to be only a first step in analysis, and even a dangerous step, when taken alone, in that it may lead people to judge irresponsibly. So he adds to his analysis his thesis of universalizability (close to implicit generality), hoping thereby to place certain responsibility-increasing constraints on our judgments. He assumes that the second part of his analysis comes *wholly as an addition* to the first part, bringing with it *new* constraints.

As I see it he is mistaken in one of two ways. Perhaps, on the one hand, he is underestimating the strength of his prescriptivism, failing to realize that it is sufficient, together with its psychological background, to imply that violations of universalizability are pointless. In that case he is also failing to realize that universalizability places no new constraints on prescriptivism. Or perhaps, on the other hand, he is assigning a special strength to universalizability (greater than I have been suggesting), thereby preventing it from being so implied by prescriptivism. In that case he is building the strong universalizability into our language in a preemptive way, by a definition that is tantamount to a value-judgment; and those who object to the special strength can be expected promptly to *build it out* of our language in order to judge *in their customary way*. Again there will be no new constraints placed on prescriptivism. I shall not attempt to decide which mistake Hare is making, for in either case the net import of his view, when corrected, will be the same as that of my emotive theory, so long as the latter is not separated, artificially, from its psychological background.

It is also true that in my previous writings I have handled universalizability (or implicit generality) in far too perfunctory a manner. Hare's work has instructively reminded me of that.

10

As I have been presenting it, the principle of implicit generality has a firm place in the theory of value; but like the ought-implies-can principle it has only a modest place. The defense that it most needs, given its philosophical history, is one that frees it from a semblance of profundity.

It retains its degree of importance insofar as it calls attention to judgments that are inadvertent. A man may judge hastily, only to find later on that he cannot generalize his judgment in a way that he considers acceptable. Since he will not repudiate the principle itself, for reasons that I have been giving, he will be inclined (apart from deception) to acknowledge that he must revise or take back his judgment. I want to emphasize that point, because my previous examples have done too little to show how the principle enters into changes and developments in a man's opinions, and may therefore have made the principle seem less important than it is.

But the principle is misconceived when it is expected to arbitrate between evaluative positions that are genuinely controversial. It cannot do that without losing its near-axiomatic plausibility. Apart from inadvertencies, both sides in any such controversy will make judgments that abide by the principle; and the reasons that both sides will need in supporting their judgments will be reasons *for approving or disapproving*—reasons that may lead men, by revealing facts, to reorganize their attitudes in a way that may alter their aims. The principle itself does not give those reasons; it does not require that those reasons must be given (for generalizations, too, can be dogmatic); it does not provide a substitute for those reasons; and it does not rule out, even, any reasons of a sort that anyone would knowingly want to give.

The principle, then, is evaluatively neutral—neutral in the sense that anyone, after only a moment's reflection, will be content to accept it, no matter whether his opinions put him in the left wing, the right wing, or the center. So perhaps I understated my case when I said, in Sidgwick's phrase, that the principle "manifestly does not give full guidance." Perhaps I should have said that it gives a guidance that is very nearly gratuitous. It simply spells out, in part, the injunction, "Be careful, in making value-judgments, to avoid talking to no purpose."

MORAL-POINT-OF-VIEW THEORIES

William K. Frankena

The expression "the moral point of view" has appeared a few times in the past twenty-five years, first in Kurt Baier's article and book of 1954 and 1958 respectively, and most recently in articles by Carole Stewart and P. W. Taylor. Much earlier it was a prominent heading in Hegel's *Phenomenology of Mind*, standing for something he was describing and attacking. Even earlier, of course, such related expressions as "the moral sense" or "the moral consciousness" appeared in Hume, Kant, and others. "The moral point of view" is not just a philosopher's phrase, for it has long been used in ordinary moral discourse too; but now it has become associated with a certain general type of ethical theory of which I am a proponent, a theory somewhat different from the kind of view Hegel excoriated.

I am asked on this occasion to discuss "the moral point of view and where [I] think that issue might be going in the next twenty-five years or so," and I take this to mean that I am to stand back a bit and take a look at what I shall call moral-point-of-view theories (MPVTs) in contemporary moral philosophy.

As a mere philosopher I shall, however, not try to don the mantle of a prophet about the future of MPVTs. Along that line I can only say that there are many types of MPVT and that, whatever may be the fate of mine, if it has any future, I cannot believe that the future of *all* of them is dark. I must admit that some of the evidence is not very encouraging: emotivism is declining but intuitionism shows signs of reviving; Hare's prescriptivism is no longer the fashion; Taylor does not get the attention he deserves; and Baier and I keep getting our ears pinned back by friends and foes alike, even by our own students. And then there's the rising influence of Quinean ways of thinking, which attack such distinctions as those between the analytic and the synthetic, the descriptive and the evaluative, the metaethical and the normative, or the moral and the nonmoral—distinctions many MPVTs trade on. Perhaps I should also mention Kuhnian ways of thinking. Besides, if someone like Gewirth or Donagan should succeed in his or her attempt to justify moral principles without bringing in the concept of the

MPV, MPVTs would become superceded, thus losing all their point. I do not expect this to happen, but it might. In any case, the best thing for me to do, it seems to me, is to address myself to the question whether we should adopt a MPVT and, if so, which.

There were MPVTs in the eighteenth century, viz. those of Hutcheson, Hume, and Adam Smith, and they recently have had a decided revival. Only a few writers have highlighted the notion of the MPV in the exact way that Baier, Taylor, and I have; but a number of others have taken a similar line, and Gewirth has grouped these together as holding a certain view about morality and the justification of moral principles, a view he regards as inadequate and seeks to displace.[1] Besides Baier, Taylor, and me he has in mind Rawls, Warnock, Nielsen, Firth, Brandt, Toulmin, and Foot; I would add Findlay (in 1944), Hare, Kemp, Kneale, M. G. Singer, and maybe Kovesi and Brennan. Many of these writers belong to what has also been called "the good reasons approach" to ethics, but perhaps not all; e.g., Hare. My own thinking along this line began a long time ago when I began to wonder about the import of the phrase, "the (or a) moral point of view," which, as I said, occurs every now and then in ordinary discourse as well as in that of philosophers who have not meant to make anything of it. In this connection, I liked very much what Royce wrote in some pages on "The Moral Insight" and James in "On a Certain Blindness in Human Beings" and "What Makes a Life Significant."[2] Could this idea be developed, I asked, and I was much encouraged in pressing my question by the appearance of Baier's article, "The Point of View of Morality," in 1954.[3] I was looking for a meta-ethical alternative to the intuitionism I was in the process of giving up, and to the emotivism I had perforce to live with. I noticed that intuitionists and emotivists alike tended not to make much distinction between moral and nonmoral judgments, attitudes, reasons, rightnesses, values, and so forth, and I hoped that making such a distinction would help me discern a new alternative. In various ways I was then put on the way to my present view by a study of the eighteenth- and twentieth-century writers already named, and, I should add, of Dewey's critique of Stevenson, H. D. Aiken's essays, papers by W. D. Falk, and P. B. Rice's *Our Knowledge of Good and Evil*. Before going on about my view, however, I must say something more about MPVTs in general and their varieties.

1

What then is a MPVT? To begin with, it is or purports to be a meta-ethical or meta-moral theory, not a normatively or substantively moral theory. It is a view *about* moral judgments and principles, about the differences between them and non-moral principles, and about the general nature of their justification. This meta-ethical theory need not as such entail subscribing to any substantive moral judgment or principle. It may entail believing that the MPV should be defined in a certain way, or that we should adopt the MPV; but, although these are normative beliefs, they are not as such or at least not necessarily moral ones. Some point of view other than the MPV may or must be taken in subscribing to them. Of course, anyone who espouses a MPVT will almost certainly also have substantive moral views, but which ones these are is not necessarily dictated by that MPVT as such.

Secondly, a MPVT gives a central place to the idea of taking the MPV. Here we must notice an ambiguity; according to Brennan,

> 'point of view' is an expression which is not only commonly used, but quite easy to understand, and I am using it in its straightforward sense.[4]

In saying this he is failing to notice that the expression has *two* "straightforward" senses. The point is that there are two ways of taking a MPV (or a scientific one, and so forth). One can do so by subscribing to a particular substantive moral principle, as Mill did when he espoused the principle of utility. Then one is taking a certain MPV—in Mill's case, that of a utilitarian. Mill might then say that from his MPV one should break a promise if doing so would mean a great increase in the general balance of happiness over unhappiness. But this is not the sense of the expression that interests MPVTs, or Brennan either. One can also take a PV in the sense of taking a general approach, perspective, stance, or vantage point from which to proceed—a PV which anyone is supposed to take who means to make judgments of a certain sort, e.g., moral ones (or scientific ones). In the former sense, taking a PV involves accepting a certain conclusion within a field or area; in the second, it involves adopting a general outlook or method that is supposed to be adopted by anyone seeking to reach conclusions in that field. Perhaps I can exhibit the distinction in this way: I once took a course called "Psychological Points of View"; in it we reviewed behaviorism, introspectionism, gestalt psychology, Freud, and so forth. A course called "The Psychological PV" would have had to be very different, if there could be such a course at all. It is a PV of the second sort—not of the first—that MPVTs are calling the MPV, as will become clearer in what follows. In fact, as we shall see, MPVTs tend to maintain that one is not taking a MPV in the first sense unless one is already taking the MPV in the second sense, more or less consciously, in arriving at it.

In order to explain further how MPVTs give an unusual role to the taking of the MPV, let me distinguish four meta-moral projects they tend to be engaged in:

(1) that of defining morality, or rather the distinction between the moral and the nonmoral;
(2) that of formulating and establishing a test for determining which moral judgments and norms are true, valid, or at least justified;
(3) that of seeing what animates morality or makes it tick; and
(4) that of showing why we should be moral.

Of these, (2), (3), and (4) are projects many sorts of moral philosophers are engaged in; (1) is more characteristic of those running MPVTs, though also pursued by others, e.g., by Gewirth. (1) is often pooh-poohed by opponents of MPVTs, e.g., by Stevenson and Peter Singer. Hume pooh-poohed it too, but at the same time he represented the affection of humanity as taking the common point of view that distinguishes morals from other kinds of evaluative discourse such as the language of self-love. Even Taylor insists that "classifying moral principles and defining the moral point of view" is important only because of "the concept of the validity of moral principles that is logically connected with it."[5] I shall not now debate the importance of project (1); I want to say only that I find it intrinsically interesting and also usefully clarifying. Even if defining the moral settles no substantive questions and so would be unimportant if all of us were clear-headed all of the time, it does not follow that one should not offer a definition of a term that is so generally and loosely used, even by those who criticize such offerings. I hope that my discussion will bear me out.

Of course, different MPVTs give different answers to the four problems, defining and bringing in the MPV in diverse ways. But all of them hold that there is such a thing as a MPV (of the second sort), a distinct and definable PV which may appropriately be called *the* MPV, and which is a single PV and not somehow a plurality or family of them. I shall call this thesis A. With it goes the view that this PV is or should be taken when we are trying to form our most *basic* moral judgments, general or particular. MPVTs usually assume that the basic judgments of morality are or should be general ones of the kind called norms, principles, rules, or standards, e.g., as Taylor does. But it is possible for a MPVT to regard particular judgments as basic, as situational moralists do. What a MPVT insists on is that we take the MPV, explicitly or implicitly, in arriving at our most basic moral judgments, whatever these are, at least when we make them first-hand. It is another matter if we simply borrow them at second-hand, for then someone else must be presumed to have taken the MPV. As for derivative moral judgments, whether these be particular or general, they do not involve taking the MPV as such; but then the MPV proper is, or is presumed to be, taken in reaching the primary moral judgments, general or particular, on which the secondary ones are based.

It should be observed that thesis A, and those to follow, can be stated either as descriptive elucidations of our actual ordinary ways of speaking and thinking in or about morality, or as proposals about how we should speak and think in or about it. MPVTs can be couched in either form; I myself prefer the second, but would, of course, hope that any such proposals I may make have a solid footing in ordinary discourse and thought, while being free of the ambiguities, vaguenesses, and other weaknesses often found there.

Certain other theses would, I believe, be accepted by all MPV theorists, though they understand them in somewhat different ways, as we shall see. I shall say, then, that, under thesis B, MPVTs hold that we can and should define morality, and the distinction between the moral and the nonmoral—i.e., between moral and nonmoral judgments, arguments, considerations, reasons, issues, uses of terms, emotions, goodnesses, rightnesses, and virtues—by some kind of reference, direct or indirect, to the MPV.[6]

Thesis C, put roughly, is the view that basic moral judgments, particular or general, may be or are to be regarded as true, valid, or at least as rationally justified if they are derived from the

MPV and after a clear-headed and full review of all that is relevant. A, B, and C, then, are in some sense the three main theses of any MPVT; but I shall also add D: that the MPV is a PV we do not necessarily take, and can reject without being inconsistent, but one which we should take. Most, if not all, MPVTs would assert it too.

Opponents of MPVTs then, will make one or more of the following claims: (1) that there is no such thing as a MPV of the sort in question (i.e., of the second sort distinguished earlier), or, if there is, it is a family or plurality of such PVs; (2) that morality and the distinction between the moral and the non-moral is impossible or unimportant to define or make, with or without reference to the MPV; (3) that basic moral judgments cannot be established as true, valid, or even justified by any rational procedure, or, if they can, this can be better done in some other way than it can by any MPVT; or (4) that we should not take the MPV, or at least that our taking it cannot be justified. Thus, "that issue" turns out to be a whole family of issues! Among these opponents, by the way, I would on one score or another list Gewirth, P. Singer, H. D. Aiken, W. D. Falk, M. G. White, D. Z. Phillips, H. O. Mounce, R. Beardsmore, C. L. Stevenson, G. H. von Wright, G. Harman, G. E. M. Anscombe, P. Geach, A. MacIntyre, and the Deweyan contextualists.

Such are the external issues between MPVTs and their opponents. There are also internal issues between proponents of different MPVTs. For theses A, B, C, and D leave open a number of questions. One is that of defining morality and the MPV, and here the main split is between those who define them in purely formal terms, as Hare does, and those who define them, at least in part, in more material or contentual terms, e.g., Toulmin. Another is the question whether use of the MPV in reaching basic moral positions, general or particular, necessarily or even always yields unique results in the sense of establishing as true, valid, or at least as justified, only one of the alternative substantive positions (all of them being moral PVs in the first of the above two senses). MPVTs all reject methodological relativism in Brandt's sense, i.e., "that there is no unique rational method in ethics"; but they may be, though they usually are not, nonmethodological relativists, holding "that there are still some instances of conflicting ethical opinions that are equally valid," as Findlay, Baier, and Brandt did, though each of them thought the instances could be limited in certain ways.[7] Even so, however, since they all include the belief "that there is a unique rational method in ethics" even if it does not always yield a unique conclusion, Gewirth is correct in seeing MPVTs as constituting a kind of "rationalism" in contemporary moral philosophy—a kind of rationalism that stands opposed, not necessarily to empiricism, but to skeptics, methodological relativists, and Stevensonian emotivists on the one hand, and to all those who believe it possible to give either an intuitive or an inferential (deductive, inductive, or dialectical) justification or proof of basic moral judgments or principles (with or without the help of definitions of ethical in non-ethical terms) on the other.

Perhaps I can highlight the significance of MPVTs in another way. It is often thought, as it was by Kant, that we are rationally justified in believing in the basic principles of our common western morality if and only if a certain general teleological, perhaps even theistic, view of man and the world is true. This teleological view is held today as a basis for ethics by Anscombe, Geach, and I think Wallace; but others reject it and yet agree that our morality can be justified only on the basis of such a view—MacIntyre and Rorty took precisely this line in a symposium in which I was involved. I take Donagan and Gewirth as trying to show that all these people are mistaken because there is an inferential way of justifying our most basic moral convictions without appealing to such a teleological premise or postulate about human nature and the universe. Now, suppose that one rejects or has doubts about that teleological picture of man and his world (one may, of course, hold it as a matter of faith rather than of reason, but then it can hardly serve as a rational basis for ethics); and that one also rejects or has doubts about the projects of Gewirth and others like him. Suppose too that one gives up the kind of autonomous justification in ethics that has been characteristic of intuitionism, namely the appeal to intuition or self-evidence. Then, it seems to me, one has but three alternatives. One is to espouse the conception of autonomous justification offered by MPVTs. The other two entail giving up on the idea of justifying our basic ethical convictions in any intuitive, inferential, or even MPVT kind of way. The one, then, opts for some sort of ethical skepticism or at least for an emotive or prescriptivist theory that does not bring in a MPV; the other chooses a kind of dogmatism, as Socrates might call it, which

gives up meta-ethics and confines itself to re-asserting and clarifying our moral value system, plus perhaps extolling its virtues
by appeal to other values we believe in that might also attract
others. The latter was Rorty's stance in the conference referred
to; I couldn't tell which of the two lines MacIntyre took.

What motivates MPVTs, in my own case and in general,
should now be clear. To return to internal issues between them,
I should like to make an interesting point. It was characteristic
of the classical meta-ethical theories of the first half of this century either not to make, or not to rest anything upon, a distinction between the moral and the nonmoral. This would be easy
to document and illustrate, but I cannot take time for that now.
It was, as I said, one of the features of that meta-ethics that came
to trouble me. It is, however, characteristic of MPVTs to make
and to rest a good deal on such a distinction, as we saw. But a
look back at my list of their exponents will show that, apart
from holding an MPVT, their meta-ethical positions are rather
varied: Findlay was an emotivist, Hare a prescriptivist, Foot and
Warnock descriptivists or neonaturalists—and then there are
Firth, Taylor, Baier, Rawls, and the others. I would like to
clarify this situation a bit by pointing out that, given the idea of
a MPV playing the roles indicated in theses B and C, it becomes
possible for the older meta-ethical views to take new (i.e.,
MPVT) forms. Thus, one can take the MPVT line and still be
an emotivist, holding either that moral judgments are expressions of a "peculiarly moral attitude" such as Stevenson regarded as unimportant, namely the MPV; or that they are expressions of attitudes that are moral because they embody the
MPV. Hutcheson and Hume, as I read them, took the first;
Smith and Findlay (and perhaps Russell) the second of these
alternatives. That is why I always felt that their kinds of "ethics
of sentiment" were more satisfactory than those of Stevenson or
Ayer. As for prescriptivism—one could subscribe to a kind of
prescriptivism analogous to the emotivism of Ayer and Stevenson without adopting the idea of a MPV and all that. Hare
seems to do this when he rejects the enterprise of distinguishing
moral and nonmoral; actually, though, especially in adding universalizability to prescriptivity and then interpreting it as he
does, he gives us a formulation of what he calls "the form of
morality" or "the moral way" that is central to the rest of his
theory, which is why I list him under the MPV theorists.[8]

Again, one can adopt the idea of a MPV and what goes with
it, and yet be a naturalist by suggesting that "morally right"

means or should be taken to mean something like "approved on careful reflection from the MPV." This is the position of Sharp and Firth. If Hutcheson and his eighteenth-century successors are not emotivists of the kind just described, then it is their position too. Most recently a somewhat different view of this sort seems to have been advocated by Rawls and Richards. Also today, there are various other kinds of descriptivism or neonaturalism, and at least some of them are MPVTs. What about intuitionism? The older intuitionism, at least in Britain, typically regarded basic moral principles as intuitively self-evident to a clarified intellect, with no requirement that any special PV be taken. But it seems to me at least theoretically possible that one might maintain that, in order to discern the basic principles or judgments of morality, one must take a special PV—namely the MPV as defined in a certain way—and that then and only then will one see that certain judgments or principles are self-evident. I do not know of anyone who maintains quite this, unless it is some of the German-speaking intuitionists; but if I may be personal again, I might admit, if pressed, that I reached my form of MPVT partly by trying to see from what PV the general principles of our morality would seem to be self-evident. What I call the principles of beneficence and equality do *seem* to me to be self-evident when I take what I conceive to be the MPV; all that keeps me from being an intuitionist of the kind in question is my doubts about any sort of intuitionist epistemology or ontology.

In any case, if the intuitionism described is a distinct possibility, then MPVTs may be emotivist, prescriptivist, intuitionist, descriptivist, naturalist, and so forth. In terms that I have used elsewhere, they can also be teleological or deontological, externalist or internalist, aretaic or deontic, and poietic or nonpoietic.

I have been laying out various kinds of points about MPVTs. Some of these points were merely expository, while others were what Mill calls considerations capable of determining the intellect to give its assent to the doctrine. Now I suppose the logical thing for me to do would be to take up in a systematic way all the issues mentioned, external or internal. I shall, however, proceed by reviewing, interpretatively and critically, the relevant works of Baier and Taylor, the two who, besides me, have been most explicitly presenting MPVTs. Then I shall continue by taking up some criticisms of such theories, especially those of Gewirth, and conclude with some statements about my own view and its problems. All of this must be done rather sketchily after this long introduction. But by doing it I can perhaps let you see the prospects for MPVTs. At least I can indicate the shape I think a MPVT should take; perhaps I can also convince you that there is a viable kind of meta-ethical theory between ethical relativism and skepticism on the one hand, and such theories as Gewirth's on the other—and that, if we despair of the latter, we need not marry the other on the rebound.

2

I have said that theses B and C can be understood in different ways, and before dealing with Baier and Taylor I must explain. The natural way to read the two theses, I think, is to take them as implying that the MPV can be defined or at least identified independently of any reference to a set of criteria for distinguishing moral judgments and norms from nonmoral ones, or for determining which moral ones are valid or justified, and hence to use them in the statement of such criteria. Assuming that we have a rough working list of moral judgments and norms to begin with, it is at least theoretically possible to do things in this way, first identifying the MPV and then propounding theses B and C straightforwardly as answers to projects (1) and (2). I am not sure that any MPV theorist has ever proceeded in this way, however, and indeed I rather doubt that it is feasible to do so. The usual procedure has been to start with a rough working list of moral judgments and norms; next, to formulate a set of criteria for distinguishing moral from nonmoral judgments and norms (perhaps also a test of validity for moral ones); and then to define the MPV by reference to them. This does not mean that MPVTs taking this approach do not subscribe to theses B and C; but it does mean that the logic of their development is not quite what those theses suggest, and that the theses may be more purely verbal than my use of them implies. I nevertheless think they furnish a useful way of picturing MPVTs, which is why I introduced them.

It is only fair from the MPV, whatever it is, to take up first Baier's article of 1954.[9] He begins by pointing out that not all advice and deliberation about what to do is moral; he says, as I would, that it is moral only if it proceeds from the MPV. What then is taking the MPV? For Baier it is trying to answer the question what to do by surveying and weighing all the relevant *moral* considerations. But what are moral considerations? His answer runs as follows: The first step in moral deliberation is to see whether one's proposed action is or is not consistent with the morality or moral rules of one's group. One is here review-ing one's action in the light of moral considerations if and only if one does this. Then, however, we must know which rules of our group are moral and which are nonmoral. Baier gives us six criteria:

> For a rule to belong to the morality of a given group it . . . is necessary . . . that it should be: (i) part of the mores of the group, (ii) supported by the characteristically moral pressure, (iii) universally teachable and therefore univer-salizable, (iv) not merely a taboo, (v) applied in accordance with certain principles of exception and modification, (vi) applied in accordance with certain principles . . . whose prevalence is a condition of the group being said to have a morality [at all].

The second step is to assess the moral rules of one's group in terms of their being "genuinely moral," i.e., true, valid, or at least morally justified. At this point Baier brings in the MPV; the rules of one's group are to be assessed from the MPV, which he defines:

> We are adopting it if we regard the rules belonging to the morality of the group as designed to regulate the behavior of people all of whom are to be treated as equally important 'centres' of cravings, impulses, desires, needs, aims, and aspirations . . . (I take this to be the meaning of 'treating them as ends in themselves and not merely as means to one's own ends').

In effect, this means for Baier that moral rules are to be judged by looking to see if they are (a) for the *good* of human beings and (b) for the good of *all* of them *alike*. That is, a rule that is a moral rule by the above six criteria is a valid moral rule if and only if it also operates for the good of all human beings alike.

It should be observed that the MPV is not mentioned in Baier's criteria for determining whether a rule is part of a mo-rality or not. But neither is the MPV defined by reference to those criteria; it is defined independently of them somehow and then brought into the business of assessing prevailing moral rules. Taking the MPV is treating persons equally as ends and not as means, or, rather, judging moral rules by the test of promoting the good of all people alike. This means that Baier may in his article be taking the first or direct approach just described. It certainly means that he affirms thesis C, and makes it look as if he would not assert B. He could, however, say that one is taking the MPV in the first step of moral deliberation if and only if one is using the moral rules of one's group in judging one's action. Then, in this step at least, taking the MPV would presuppose one's knowing which of the prevailing rules are moral ones; hence, the MPV would not be independently definable, and so far Baier would be taking the second or more usual approach. He could also so far accept thesis B, at least verbally. *Qua* separately definable, the MPV would appear only in the second step.

There are several things that worry me about Baier's position in his article, as just presented. (a) I do not see that, even in the first step of applying rules or standards to one's actions in particular cases, one is taking the MPV if and only if one is judging by reference to the morality prevailing in one's group. One is, it seems to me, taking the MPV here even if one is applying only one's own moral principles, whether these are also those of one's group or not. Baier recognized this later in his book: "A person has adopted the moral point of view when he reviews the facts in the light of *his* moral convictions."[10] (b) It seems to me that Taylor is right in accusing Baier of ethnocentricity in bringing equality into the definition of the MPV at the second step, and so into the test for determining whether inequalitarian moralities are valid or not. This strikes me as begging the question against such moralities. (c) It is not clear how Baier arrives at the definition of the MPV as used in the assessment of moral codes; it seems to appear out of the blue. (d) He does not seem here to allow for the existence of nonhuman "centres" of cravings, impulses, and so forth, as I think one should.

What Baier does in his book is very different. Again he is asking: what are moral reasons or considerations? He takes it to be part of the idea of morality that moral convictions, rules, and the like are true or false, and appears to hold that a consideration or reason is a moral one if and only if it is based on a true moral principle. Thus he does not describe the first step in moral deliberation as he did in the article; instead he describes it as indicated in the last sentence quoted. But in doing so he implies that one is not then really taking the MPV if one's moral convictions are not true. "In such a case, [one] merely *means* to adopt the moral point of view, but has not succeeded."[11] This strikes me as decidedly odd. In any case, Baier is particularly concerned to argue that there is a test of truth in morality and that it is or involves the MPV. " . . . our moral convictions are true if they can be seen to be required or acceptable *from the moral point of view.*"[12] The central problem, then, is that of defining the MPV. "When we adopt a certain point of view, we adopt its defining principle."[13] What then is the defining principle of the MPV for Baier? It is decidedly not the principle of self-interest in any of its forms, direct or indirect. Rather, one is taking the MPV when, besides not being egoistic, one is doing things on principle, willing to universalize one's principles, and considering the good of everyone alike in formulating them. Notice here, that this complex "defining principle" is not just a criterion for determining which of one's principles are moral or nonmoral; it is this, but it is also a criterion for telling which of them are true and which not.

So, which approach is Baier taking and which theses does he assert? He certainly is asserting A and, at least verbally, C—perhaps B also. But he is now defining the MPV in terms of a set of criteria for determining which basic convictions are (a) moral and (b) true, or either. Since this is so, what is logically basic for Baier is the discernment of these criteria, not the identification of the MPV, and his approach is of the second or more usual sort. What then of projects (3) or (4)? In the article it appears as if what makes morality tick for Baier is a basic attitude of seeing people (equally) as ends and not as means. Perhaps the same is true of his view in the book; but there he stresses the claim that "morality is designed to apply in just . . . those [cases] where interests conflict," saying in fact that "by 'the moral point of view' we *mean* a point of view which furnishes a court of arbitration for conflicts of interest."[14] As for project (4), this is hardly broached in the article, but is a main concern of the book. Here Baier equates the questions why one should adopt the MPV and why one should be moral, and answers them by giving a Hobbesian kind of argument:[15]

> We should be moral because being moral is following rules designed to overrule reasons of self-interest whenever it is in

the interest of everyone alike that such rules should be generally followed.[16]

Some of the criticisms made earlier apply here also, namely (b) and (d), perhaps also (c), though to a lesser degree. I should like to add (e) that Baier here does not sufficiently distinguish the question why we should be moral rather than nonmoral from the question why we should be moral rather than immoral, and (f) that he also over-conflates asking which norms are moral and asking which moral norms are true or valid [i.e., projects (1) and (2)]. It seems to me important to keep these projects apart and not to beg either question in pursuing them.

3

Taylor, too, has put forward two MPVTs, one in his unduly neglected book and another in a more recent article.[17] I shall consider what he does in the book first, limiting myself to what is directly relevant. Here he is certainly espousing theses A and B, arguing in fact that moral "values" are best distinguished by reference to the PV involved. Yet he is taking my second approach, not the first. For he thinks of the moral realm of normative discourse as defined and governed (a) by the "rules of inference" common to all realms of normative discourse, and (b) by the "rules of relevance" that characterize the moral realm. A judgment or norm is moral or nonmoral if and only if it belongs to the realm of normative discourse governed by certain rules of relevance. Taylor does not say in the book what these rules of relevance are, though it is interesting that he calls them rules of *relevance*. He tells us only that formulating them is a task for philosophical analysis or "explication." It is clear that he means to distinguish them from basic moral principles; it is not clear whether he thinks they must be purely formal or not, though his criticisms of Baier suggest that he does. He explicitly denies, however, that moral norms by definition take precedence over others or are held to with a deeper commitment.[18] I agree with this, as will appear, though many moral philosophers would not; but I wish to remark that it still may be that one who takes the MPV and means to be moral (as versus immoral) must regard moral considerations as at least normally outweighing nonmoral, e.g., prudential, ones. At any rate, for Taylor, the rules of relevance are not stated in terms of the MPV; rather, the MPV is defined by reference to them. To take the MPV just is to decide to adopt the appropriate rules of relevance.[19] Taylor can thus subscribe to thesis B and does, but only with this point understood.

I should at this point say a little about Taylor's conception of the kind of philosophical explication that would be involved in stating the rules of relevance for the moral realm. It is not just a matter of describing rules governing the way people think in morality. The canons of moral reasoning defining the MPV do, he believes, have an empirical base in the way people actually think, but the canons are themselves normative: "they are *guides* for people to follow in their reasoning."[20] They are rules which one must follow if one is to be fully rational in thinking about moral matters. I couldn't agree more.

But now Taylor makes a surprising move. He does not assert thesis C; he *denies* it. Taking up the question of justifying a basic moral norm or "value," he does not bring in the MPV as playing any part at all. He argues that "in order to justify a particular value system (which belongs to a point of view) we must step *outside* the point of view."[21] To justify it we must step outside the moral realm into a "whole way of life" chosen under certain conditions, that is, being free, enlightened, and impartial. This means that for Taylor the MPV is a fifth wheel in the process of justification; for, by his own logic, if it is not involved in justifying one moral value system (MVS) as against another, then it is not involved in justifying any moral norm or judgment. Here, however, I believe that he was simply making a mistake in terms of his own theory. For even on his own view, taking the MPV is just adopting certain unstated rules of relevance that are common to all MVSs, in addition to the rules of inference governing all normative discourse. But, if these rules of relevance are supposed to underlie all MVSs, then it is in principle possible to use them in arguing for one MVS and against another; one need not even at this stage step outside the MPV and the rules defining it. It may be, for instance, that the rules of moral relevance are more faithfully observed in, or better fulfilled by, one MVS than another; whether this is so or not depends on what the defining principles of the MPV are, of course, but it is a possibility that Taylor simply ignores (and one that is central to my own theory).

In discussing the justification of basic moral norms, Taylor in his book was not making enough of a distinction between the

question of justifying one MVS over another, a question internal to the moral realm, and other more properly external questions. Dealing with the topic of "justifying the MPV," Taylor
distinguishes three such external questions:

(a) that of justifying one's account of what the MPV is, i.e.,
justifying one's account of the canons of moral reasoning;
(b) that of justifying taking the MPV, i.e., justifying adopting and using the canons of moral reasoning, i.e., justifying being moral as versus non-moral;
(c) that of justifying being moral as versus immoral.

What he says about (a) I have already indicated. About (b) he
again does something surprising. He alleges that, given an answer to (a), (b) is easy to answer, because the canons in question
are precisely those that should govern the business of making
such judgments, since they define what it is to be rational in
doing so. They tell us

how we would think (upon adopting [the moral] point of
view) if we were fully rational.
. . . the decision to take a point of view is *always* justified.
It is the decision to commit oneself to an ideal of rationality.
Deciding to adopt a point of view is deciding to follow the
canons which define what it means to reason in the best
(i.e., the most rational) way possible.
   Another way to put this is as follows. What an accurate
explication explicates is the ideal to which everyone who
takes a certain point of view is committed in the act of
taking it. To take the moral point of view . . . is to commit
oneself to the ideal of always giving good and relevant reasons when justifying moral judgments, moral prescriptions,
moral standards, and moral rules. . . . The decision to
take the moral point of view is simply the decision to be as
rational as one can concerning moral matters. Such a decision is justified precisely because this is what the decision
consists in.[22]

This sounds so right, but something funny is going on. For
adopting the MPV is not just adopting the rules for reasoning
and judging rationally in a certain area. It is more like deciding
to enter that area in the first place, and this is a different busi-

ness, at least if we can opt not to make moral judgments at all, as Taylor and I both think we can. For then we might opt not to go in for "moral matters," and, if we did, there would be no question of our being or not being rational about them. To take the MPV is not just to decide to be rational in making moral judgments or reaching moral conclusions; it includes deciding to make moral judgments (to become a moral judge, as Taylor puts it), and one cannot make *moral* judgments unless one is taking the MPV. Of course, the canons defining the MPV tell us how we would think *if* we adopted the MPV *and* were fully rational; but explicating and establishing those canons does not yet show us that we should adopt it or them.

While Taylor is correct in distinguishing questions (b) and (c) more clearly than Baier does, he should have seen, as Baier did, that (b) is much like (c). In dealing with (c), he saw that answering it does entail stepping out of every MVS and out of the MPV itself and, in fact, into a more ultimate PV—that involved in asking how it is rational *sans phrase* to live. He does not try to answer this question, but he does in my opinion do a fine job of explicating its logic when he equates it with asking how one would choose to live if one were ideally free, enlightened, and impartial. The question whether one should adopt any MVS at all, take the MPV, or be moral is then the question whether one would choose to do so if one were in such an ideal state of rationality. It is not the question whether it is in one's interest to be moral in any of these ways, as so many have supposed—nor is it even Baier's question whether living in a certain way is in the interest of everyone alike, oneself included, which is still a kind of prudential question. It is more like Thornton's question how one *most wants* to live, which is not necessarily prudential, as he points out; but it represents the right way to ask *that* question, as Thornton's wording does not.[23]

Taylor's position in his 1978 article, "On Taking the Moral Point of View," is rather different.[24] Without talking about rules of relevance, he now offers us definitions of morality and of the MPV that are much like Baier's, but he rejects the charge of ethnocentricity, possibly because of Nielsen's reply to it.[25] First, then, he gives us a test for determining whether a norm is or is not a moral one (i.e., belongs to the category of morality). It does, if and only if it has the following characteristics:

(1) it is general in form;
(2) it is understood as universal in scope;

(3) it is intended to function as an overriding norm;

(4) it is intended to be disinterested or categorical in the sense of applying irrespective of an agent's desires or interests;

(5) it is intended to function as a public norm;

(6) it is substantively impartial, or such that, when it is adopted and applied, equal consideration is given to every person as a person.

The last clause Taylor expressly equates with Baier's requirement that moral norms must be "for the good of everyone alike," and is intended to rule out Hare's "fanatics." He correctly observes that by this test a norm may be a moral one without being acceptable, justified, true, or validly binding. For acceptability or validity some further test is necessary. He then claims that because this is so, we can

> . . . avoid any sort of ethnocentric fallacy. Even if the test for classifying norms as moral ones includes characteristics that are found only in the actual morality of one's own culture, as long as we do not use these criteria of classification as themselves constituting grounds of validity no fallacy need be involved.[26]

Here I must demur again. The point in Taylor's last sentence is correct; but, for all that, if one's definition of morality includes features present only in our own morality, then the codes or value systems of other cultures cannot be moralities, and the definition is ethnocentric after all. And in including clause (6), Taylor's definition *is* ethnocentric in this sense. We both see no reason why morality should be defined so broadly that every individual or society has a morality no matter what the form or content of his, her, or its action-guide may be. But I believe that one restricts the denotation of "morality" unduly if one insists that an action-guide must give *equal* consideration to all people or persons if it is to be a morality; to refer to Taylor's own earlier article, such a restriction rules out of morality (not as immoral but as nonmoral) all value systems that sanction castes, slavery, and so forth.[27] I submit, therefore, that clause (6) is too strong, though I shall myself come out with something very close to it.

Most of Taylor's other clauses I would accept, I think; however, for reasons that I have given elsewhere, I reject his priority clause [i.e., (3)]. He and I agree that it is not a sufficient condition of an action-guide being moral that it be taken as supremely authoritative, but he now is making it a necessary condition, as he did not earlier. Even about this I have doubts. We do not always take moral considerations as overriding all others when they come into conflict, and we sometimes speak of religion, say, as transcending or even suspending morality or the ethical. We may not be correct in this, but we are not talking nonsense. I have also argued in the past that putting a priority clause in the definition of morality begs the question why we should take the MPV or be moral. But Taylor reasons convincingly that it does not:

> It might appear to do so since, according to [it], moral principles must by definition take priority over all other principles. This appearance is dispelled, however, when we see that the question, why should one take the moral point of view? is equivalent to asking: What reasons justify a person's accepting principles from a point of view that entails the supremacy of moral reasons-for-acting? In this question a moral reason-for-acting is understood to be any reason-for-acting grounded on a normative principle having the *five* characteristics of generality, universality, disinterestedness, publicity, and impartiality. It is not logically necessary that principles having these *five* characteristics also have the characteristic of priority. . . . Because the priority is a *sixth* independent characteristic, the possibility of providing a justification for the moral point of view remains open. Such a justification would require that one show why principles having the *five* characteristics mentioned above ought to be adopted as the supreme norms of practical reason in the rational decision-making of all moral agents.[28]

His wording is misleading but his point is at least partly correct. I would prefer to read the question of why we should take the MPV as asking why we should adopt a set of principles fulfilling all *six* of his conditions (or whatever conditions one takes as defining the moral); but the effect is much the same.

The six criteria are not as such a definition of the MPV but of morality, or, rather, of the class of moral norms. Since they are stated without reference to the MPV, Taylor is clearly taking my second approach. In fact, he now goes on to state a test for the validity or justifiability of moral norms, also without mentioning the MPV. In doing so he associates himself with "the recent revival of the Kantian tradition in ethics" led by Baier, Rawls, and Richards. He calls his test "the ideal mutual agreement test" (IMAT):

> . . . a rule or standard is a valid moral principle if and only if it would be subscribed to under ideal conditions of freedom, rationality, and factual knowledge by all autonomous agents as one of their publicly recognized and mutually acknowledged overriding norms.[29]

With these two tests formulated—one for determining which norms are moral and the other for determining which moral norms are valid—Taylor then, and only then, proceeds to define the MPV, doing so in two stages. The first is to define taking it in what he calls "the first context," i.e., in the business of making particular moral judgments where one is applying norms to particular cases. To take the MPV in this context is to apply norms that (a) one takes to be moral, which entails implicitly or explicitly accepting the six criteria listed earlier, and (b) one takes to be valid or justified. The second context is that in which we are assessing norms themselves to see whether they are moral and valid and so acceptable for application in contexts of the first sort. To take the MPV in this context is to adopt and use both of the tests already described: the six-criteria test of morality and the IMA test of validity.

Taking the MPV is thus defined by Taylor in terms of adopting not just a test of morality, but also a test of validity—not the other way around as theses B and C suggest. Nevertheless, he can subscribe to these theses at least in words, since he holds that there is a necessary equivalence between taking the MPV and adopting those tests. Now, I agree with part of Taylor's procedure, for I believe that one must first define the distinction between moral and nonmoral judgments, and so forth, which I do mainly in terms of the kinds of reasons that are or would be given for them, then defining or describing the MPV on the basis of what one comes out with. But Taylor also makes prior acceptance of an IMAT a condition for taking the MPV, and this bothers me. I agree that in morality we make a claim to the validity or justifiability of our judgments and norms, and that an IMAT of some sort is involved in this claim. And I see no objection to defining taking the MPV as involving a claim to the justifiability or validity of one's judgments and norms. But it seems to me possible and desirable to identify the MPV without reference to any particular kind of validity test, i.e., to define or describe it by reference to the kinds of facts taken to be reasons for what one says. This is why I like Taylor's earlier talk about defining the MPV in terms of rules of *relevance*. I should therefore prefer to state the kind of an IMAT that is involved in a MPVT as follows: a moral judgment or norm is justified if and only if it would be subscribed to under ideal conditions of freedom, rationality, imagination, and factual knowledge by all who take the MPV. Then the test of morality is prior to the MPV but the MPV is prior to the IMAT. And thesis C can be taken at its face value, even if B cannot.

About Taylor's IMAT—though he does not say so in the last statement quoted, he must be maintaining that a moral rule or standard is valid only if all autonomous agents under the ideal conditions mentioned agree to it as satisfying his six criteria. This means, in the first place, that these agents must see the rule or standard as being "such that, when it is adopted and applied, equal consideration is given to every person as a person."[30] But then he is using his sixth criterion as itself constituting a test of validity, and is after all being ethnocentric—not only in his definition of morality (as I argued earlier), but in the sense in which he claimed not to be when he rejected the charge of committing the ethnocentric fallacy. It means, in the second place, that even to be a valid moral norm, a norm must be agreed to by all of said agents as having priority over all nonmoral ones. This may not be ethnocentric, but it does seem to be too strong. To be sure, one can ask of a norm that is in fact valid by the IMAT why one should live by it, if one does not oneself see it as passing that test. But one cannot oneself see it as passing that test, and so as, among other things, having priority over other norms and considerations, and still ask why one should live by it. In this sense, one cannot ask why one should be moral after all, even if one can ask it in the sense explained earlier. One certainly cannot ask why one should do what one knows to be right, as Taylor in his book rightly thinks one can.

In his book Taylor carefully distinguished the questions: (a) Why ought I to be moral? (b) Why ought I to take the MPV?; and I assume he still means to do so, though some of what he says in answering (b) will also apply to (a). But here he does not answer (b) in the way I complained about earlier. He argues, first, that, if one accepts the six criteria for moral norms, then one is committed to accepting his IMAT view of moral validity. I suppose he would claim more generally that, if one accepts any set of criteria for moral norms, one must then also accept a corresponding IMAT of moral validity. I am not convinced by this claim, partly because I fail to see that merely agreeing that a norm is moral if it fulfills N conditions commits one to any view about the test of its validity, or even to a belief that it is valid. Taylor's real point is that, if one asks whether a norm that fulfills the conditions for being moral is also valid, or if one claims that it is valid, as one does if one accepts it, then one is raising a question that can only be answered by accepting the corresponding form of IMAT—and this point seems to me to be correct. What really interests me here, however, is the second part of his argument—that anyone who takes the MPV in the second context (i.e., who adopts his six criteria and his IMAT in the business of classifying and assessing norms) must be making a certain "prior" commitment, one which is then "a necessary condition for taking the MPV." This prior commitment is the attitude of equal respect for all persons, or a belief in their having equal intrinsic worth (or having equal basic rights). To justify my taking the MPV finally requires, then, justifying my adopting this attitude. But this attitude, Taylor says, is an "ultimate" one, one for or against which no reasons can be given.[31] It is then not rationally required, but it is not irrational either. One must simply decide, when the full nature of the choice is faced, whether or not to commit oneself to taking this attitude toward persons; and, if I may bring the book in here, one's decision is rational if it is ideally free, enlightened, and impartial, if it is the decision one would make if one were ideally free, enlightened, and impartial.

Now, I accept Taylor's equalitarianism and its tenet of the equal intrinsic worth of persons—but, as I have already indicated, I do not believe that we should build it into the definition of morality or of the MPV, or make it a precondition of taking the MPV. To do so is to deny that anyone who asserts that people do not have equal inherent value can have a morality or take the MPV, when it seems appropriate to say only that a person making such an assertion has a mistaken morality or sees through the moral glass too darkly. I should also not want to say, as Taylor does, that no reasons can be given for or against taking the MPV. Otherwise I believe that Taylor here at the end comes close to the truth about the MPV, about what it is and why one should take it—provided we leave the word "equal" out of it. In fact, rather than defining the MPV as Taylor does and then saying that it has as its precondition the attitude of equal respect for all persons, I would want to identify taking the MPV as including having respect for human beings or persons, and not for them only but also for other consciously sentient beings capable of suffering. It finally just is—or almost is—this attitude and the "insight" Royce and James associate with it. It entails ascribing intrinsic worth, though not necessarily equal intrinsic worth, to all persons. Even if those who take the MPV and are free, rational, and factually enlightened, will agree that they all, or at least all persons, have equal inherent value, this conclusion should not be made a part of its definition. Here I take believing in the intrinsic worth of persons and other conscious sentient beings to be the same thing as believing that there are ways of treating them that are right or wrong, good or bad, just because they are what they are, independently of an agent's own desires or interests. Putting it in another way, I hold that the actions of moral agents are made morally right, wrong, good, bad, and so forth, by certain sorts of facts about what they do to conscious sentient beings as such, whether in one's own person or in that of another—if I may echo Kant's second form of the supreme principle of morality, which also comes close to the truth.

4

Gewirth is an equalitarian, as Taylor and I are; indeed, his interest is primarily in "the justification of the principles of an egalitarian-universalist morality."[32] Like us, too, he wants to avoid ethnocentricity and question-begging in the definition of morality and the MPV, and in the justification of moral principles. But he believes that his view does this better than *any* MPVT can, and that he can give a more solid kind of justification for equalitarianism or any moral principle than others can:

A definitive justification of a supreme moral principle must provide, in a way that does not beg the question, determinate and conclusive answers to the . . . questions of moral philosophy . . . such answers are to be obtained through

an analysis of certain considerations about reason and action, as these considerations are reflected in their respective
concepts.[33]

They cannot be obtained by any kind of use of "the MPV." As I
have already intimated, if he is right, MPVTs, however well
they may be worked out, lose all their appeal, for then we have
something better. Here, however, I cannot discuss his own alternative theory of justification, which I find dubious; I must
confine myself to reviewing his points about MPVTs. But I hope
by doing this to support my conviction that, if no such better
alternative is available, then we may and should take the
MPVT line for at least "the next 25 years or so."

In his discussions of MPVTs Gewirth is operating with a definition of morality and the moral, which he makes explicit in
his book:

> . . . morality has a unique status. For it purports to set, for
> everyone's conduct, requirements that take precedence over
> all other modes of guiding action, including even the self-
> interest of the persons to whom it is addressed . . . from
> among the diverse meanings of 'morality' and 'moral' a cer-
> tain core meaning may be elicited. According to this, a
> morality is a set of categorically obligatory requirements for
> action that are addressed at least in part to every actual or
> prospective agent, and that are concerned with furthering
> the interests, especially the most important interests, of
> persons or recipients other than or in addition to the agent
> or the speaker.[34]

This definition is rightly more neutral than Baier's or Taylor's,
for it does not build equalitarianism into the very meaning of
"morality." It can also be read as being neutral as between
teleological and deontological moralities (as it should be), and as
leaving open the question whether all human beings or only
some (besides the agent or the speaker) are morally considerable, as well as the question whether other sentient beings are.
All this is as it should be, though I am not sure I want to make
"interests" as central to the definition of morality as he does (he
does explicitly leave the question of the nature of "interests"
open). In fact, his definition of morality is much like the one I
once gave,[35] except that he builds in the idea of "furthering" the

interests, especially "the most important interests" of other persons or recipients, thus running a risk of not being neutral enough. My main question about Gewirth's definition concerns his inclusion of the clause that moral requirements take precedence over all others, about which I have already commented. He might even be willing to define the MPV as the PV that is implied in this definition, thus accepting thesis B as well as A, and rejecting only C and D, which are his real targets.

Gewirth's discussion of MPVTs comes in bits and pieces in his first chapter. Just before the first piece he points out that people hold conflicting moral beliefs and that there is a problem about determining which are true, since they cannot be checked with empirical facts as scientific statements can. Then:

> If it is replied . . . that the moral statement is true if it conforms to or is derivable from the 'moral point of 'view,' this has the difficulties that there may be quite opposed moral points of view and that the moral point of view in its favored egalitarian-universalist interpretation must itself receive adequate justification if it is to justify such judgments.[36]

This passage, cryptic and hard to assess, seems to trade on the ambiguity of the phrase "moral point of view" that I pointed out at the beginning. Of course, there are opposed moral points of view in the first sense. But, if one defines the MPV in the second sense in the way suggested by Gewirth's own definition of morality, then there are not. Again, he is, of course, right in saying that there is a problem even about justifying the MPV if it is defined in an egalitarian-universalist way, as by Baier and Taylor. But is there the same sort of problem about justifying the MPV if it is defined in the neutral way suggested by his own definition of morality—or in the ways in which it is defined, say, by Hare or me?

The second piece appears when Gewirth takes up views maintaining that there is no problem about justifying certain basic moral principles since they belong to the concept of morality itself.[37] He quotes Baier as giving this status to a kind of equalitarianism and Foot as doing so for a concern for well-being, and then says (a) that if they are using "moral" as meaning the opposite of "immoral," then they are begging questions against those who hold other views about what is right or wrong; and (b) that if they mean to use "moral" in its descriptive or neutral sense as the opposite of "nonmoral", then they should not define it so as to make nonmoral the views of all those who reject equalitarianism or a concern for well-being. In both these comments Gewirth is correct, according to me, but they leave untouched such MPVTs as Hare's and mine. He goes on to find a further difficulty in the theories in question, namely, (c) that they leave unanswered the question as to why one should be moral in the sense in which they define this term, i.e., why one should live by the principles built into their definitions. Again, Gewirth is correct in saying that the MPVTs in question must face this problem. But have they no possible answer? Suppose that Baier or Foot is right in regarding his or her "substantive content" as part of the very definition of "moral" (as opposed to "non-moral"), and can show this by some kind of philosophical explication in Taylor's sense, independently of showing us that we should act in accordance with that substantive content. It seems in principle possible that one could do this. But if one succeeds, then one has both justified one's definition and established a certain "substantive" principle *as a principle of morality.* Of course, it can still be asked why we should be moral, which will include acting in accordance with this principle. But asking *this* is asking whether it is rational for one to be moral in the sense defined—and this question is still open. However, it may be that Baier or Foot has a satisfactory answer to it; their actual answers are not adequate, as has often been pointed out, but it is at least in principle possible for them to have an adequate answer. Even if they do not, this fact by itself is no objection to his or her definition as such, or even to the claim that said principle is by definition a principle of morality.

Building such material clauses into the very concept of morality is objectionable only if doing so begs the question of whether or not some value-system that is plausibly regarded as a morality is in fact one. I agree with Gewirth that both Baier's and Foot's definitions are not neutral enough in this sense, though I agree with them—and him—that a material clause should be part of the definition of morality. This, then, is the issue—this, and the question whether such MPVTs, or any others, can explain why we should be moral.

Gewirth then attacks Rawls' particular kind of MPVT as involving a circle, but I shall not comment on this. Next he criticizes theories seeking to justify a moral principle by using "a reflexive method," i.e., theories that hold a moral principle is justified because it would be chosen under certain conditions, e.g., ideal observer theories and MPVTs.[38] He describes them as "inductive," but this is hardly right, since they do not typically think of the process involved as an inference, either inductive or deductive. All of them, he alleges, suffer from a "fatal dilemma" because the statements of the conditions of choice, e.g., being free, fully informed, impartial, willing to universalize, considering the good of everyone alike, and so forth, must be either morally neutral or morally normative. If the latter, then the procedure is circular or question-begging. If the former, then "there is no guarantee that such non-moral traits will lead to the selection of one moral principle as against another, or in particular to an egalitarian-universalist principle." All of this a MPV theorist must simply admit. But one may still insist that no such deductive proof of certain moral principles as Gewirth is looking for is available—and also that whether a neutrally defined MPV will lead to the selection of a certain set of moral principles as against all others depends on how it is defined. Some definitions are more hopeful than others without being circular or question-begging, though for none of them is there any guarantee of unique results—or that nonmethodological relativism is false. Hare at least has argued that his kind of reflexive method, which centers on the principle of universalizability, is both neutral and leads univocally to a utilitarian conclusion. He may be wrong, but he is in principle possibly correct. For that matter, is it so obvious that one who defined the MPV in accordance with Gewirth's definition of morality would be mistaken in believing that all those who genuinely take that PV and are free, clear-headedly rational, and fully knowledgeable, will agree on certain principles? Of course, none of this is worth wasting time on if it is clear, as it is to Gewirth, that there is a conclusive inferential proof of some moral principles. But what if this isn't clear?

When he comes to introducing his own alternative theory Gewirth argues that the supreme principles of morality must be materially as well as formally necessary, since, by the definition of morality, they must apply to or be binding on moral agents independently of their own desires or interests. The implication is that MPVTs cannot provide for the categorical character of moral principles. H. D. Aiken has pressed the same point, though against the background of a kind of personal voluntarism that is poles apart from Gewirth's position, so far away that if Aiken's view were true, Gewirth and Kant alike would deny that moral principles could be categorically binding on any

agent other than the one who espouses them. Even on him they
are binding only if or because he adopts them "in conscience,"
which hardly makes them categorical in any sense that a MPVT
cannot provide for. Be this as it may, *are* moral principles by
definition categorical in application and bindingness, and *does* a
MPVT necessarily make them hypothetical? This is a large
order, but I must be brief. Discussing the first question, Quinton contends that there are some irreducibly categorical moral
injunctions and some hypothetical ones, but he is not using
these terms in Kant's senses. Using the same terms approxi-
mately in Kant's senses, Foot has maintained that morality is or
rather should be a system of hypothetical imperatives. I have
opposed her in this, because I believe, as Baier and Taylor do,
that there are right and wrong ways for me to treat persons and
sentient beings just because of what they are, independently of
my own desires and interests, and independent even of my
taking the MPV; and I have already suggested that believing
this is part of taking the MPV. I would not accept such obligations if I did not take the MPV, but I have them anyway, and it
is part of the MPV to see it thus. Genuinely hypothetical imperatives in Kant's sense are calculated and understood not to
apply to an agent unless that agent has certain desires or interests; but this is not so for moral ones, and I see no reason why
a MPVT cannot agree to and even insist on this. Morality, on
my view, as much as on Gewirth's, sees its requirements as

> . . . categorically obligatory in that compliance with them
> is mandatory for the conduct of every person to whom they
> are addressed regardless of whether he wants to accept them
> or their results, and regardless also of the requirements of
> any other institutions such as law or etiquette. . . .[39]

It says, as it were, speaking from the MPV, "You ought to do so-
and-so independently of your desires or point of view"; it does
not say "If and only if you take the MPV, then you ought to do
so-and-so"; nor does it say "You ought to do so-and-so" with
the understanding that you need not if you are not taking the
MPV.

In effect, I am agreeing with Taylor, Baier, and Gewirth that
basic moral Oughts are by definition categorical or at least nonhypothetical in the sense of being intended as norms to be applied and complied with irrespective of the agent's inclinations,
interests, or point of view. As Taylor puts the matter,

To take the moral point of view is to adopt and apply stand-ards or rules 'categorically', disregarding whatever conse-quences they might have for furthering or frustrating our ends (other than the end of acting morally).

. . . To adopt a moral norm is to subscribe to a principle that is intended to be applied disinterestedly *by all moral agents*.

. . . a moral norm [is] one that is intended to be applied by each agent to himself or herself as a matter of principle."[40]

But for this to cover the whole point, it must be added that for morality a person is a moral agent and is addressed by its norms even if she or he does not take the MPV.

However, it remains true, as Aiken and Gewirth might and as Foot certainly would insist, that such nonhypothetical moral Oughts, though applying to and being seen as categorically binding on all persons, may not actually *be* binding on a person who does not take the MPV, or on anyone for that matter, in the sense of being irrational to ignore or contravene. Even Kant, whether he is interpreted as running a MPVT or not, recognized this in a way when he contended that one can ra-tionally obey the categorical imperatives of morality only under the postulate that there is a God who will apportion happiness to moral virtue. This is, of course, precisely why Gewirth, as op-posed to MPVTs, Aiken, and maybe Kant, seeks for a new way to justify basic moral norms. But, as I suggested earlier, it must not simply be assumed that it is impossible for a MPVT to show that it is irrational not to be moral; and if it can do so, then its Oughts will be as categorical as can be. MPVTs are not quite so easily disposed of as their opponents think.

5

I have reviewed the MPVTs proposed by Baier and Taylor and some criticisms of MPVTs in general by Gewirth and others. In the course of doing so I have given a number of indi-cations of the kind of MPVT I have been proposing, and I turn now to presenting it a little more systematically and saying something about some of its problems, all rather briefly.

It has always seemed to me that definitions of morality and the MPV should be neutral, more neutral than those of Baier, Taylor, or Foot. Hare, Gewirth, and others are right about this. Such definitions should cover all action and life-guides that are plausibly called moralities, whether teleological or deontological, equalitarian or nonequalitarian, aretaic or deontic—though I see no objection to ruling out "ethical" egoism and aestheticism, provided it is understood that doing so only declassifies them as moralities and does nothing to show that one should not live by them. For various reasons, often advanced by myself and others, I find purely affective and formal definitions unsatisfactory, and so believe that a material clause must be included, besides affective or formal ones or both. Such a material clause must not only specify the subjects of moral judgments, that is, persons or rational beings, their actions, traits, motives, intentions, and so forth; it must also distinguish between moral and other evaluative or normative judgments about them by indicating the kinds of considerations, facts, or reasons that are or are to be taken as *relevant* to the making of such judgments. Considerations or reasons for evaluative or normative judgments are moral, in my opinion, if and only if they consist ultimately of facts of a certain sort, namely facts about what acts, agents, traits, and so forth do or are intended to do to persons or conscious sentient beings or both as such, including others besides the agent or speaker in question; e.g., facts about whether such beings are or are intended to be caused to suffer, to have their interests fulfilled or frustrated, to have true or false beliefs, or to have better or worse lives, or shorter ones. Other kinds of facts are irrelevant unless they are connected with facts of these sorts, as of course they often are. I thus arrive at a test for distinguishing moral judgments from other normative or evaluative ones. The test consists of a material clause of the sort just indicated, plus some formal clauses such as the prescriptivity and universalizability requirements stressed by Hare and the nonhypotheticalness discussed earlier.

It is often thought that any view taking it as part of the concept of morality that certain kinds of facts and not others are relevant to moral issues is necessarily morally non-neutral—that it is in effect laying down a certain substantive moral principle and precluding others. This is not so. A substantive moral principle always says that a certain fact or kind of fact is a significant or even conclusive reason for a certain moral judgment or kind of judgment, e.g., that the fact that x *harms someone* is such a reason for judging that x is *wrong*. But my kind of material clause says nothing like this. It does not say *which* facts are relevant in *which* way to *which* judgments; it says only that the facts that are relevant to moral judgments *in one way or another* are facts of a certain sort or family of sorts. In effect, it says that, for a principle to be a substantive moral one, it must select some fact or kind of fact from the range assigned by it and tell us what moral judgment it is a reason for. It does not itself do this. It cannot therefore commit me to one moral principle or value-system as opposed to another, though I do maintain that taking the MPV, neutral as it is, will in fact lead one to accept some principles rather than others.

Next to the question of including a material criterion in the definition of "moral" as versus "nonmoral," comes that of including a formal priority clause such as is used by Taylor (in his article) and Gewirth. I did include such a clause in the Colorado version of my "The Concept of Morality" but took it out of the later *Journal of Philosophy* version; I shall here say no more about it than I already have; in general, I am convinced by such reasons for excluding it as have been given by Taylor (in his book), Warnock, and Quinton.[41]

Thus far, in stating my view, I have not mentioned the MPV; I am distinguishing the moral from the nonmoral without referring to it, taking what I earlier called the second approach. I do, however, want to define or at least identify the MPV with the help of the criteria used in making the distinction, especially the criterion describing the kinds of facts that are relevant to moral judgments, though, as against Taylor and perhaps Baier, without making reference to any test or criterion of justifiability, validity, or truth. Roughly, I wish to define or at least describe the MPV as that which is taken if or when one makes evaluative and normative judgments about persons on the basis of facts of the sorts indicated. I can then still subscribe to thesis B, as I mean to, at least verbally. In doing this I am talking mainly about taking the MPV in what Taylor calls the second context; unlike him, however, I want for present purposes to allow for "situational" views, which regard particular moral judgments as basic, as well as for views that hold general moral norms (rules, principles, standards, and so forth) to be fundamental. I shall therefore ignore Taylor's distinction in what I say here; it must not be forgotten, but it is easy to provide for when needed.

Before going on, I must distinguish two things or states of mind. The first is just agreeing that a certain set of criteria does serve satisfactorily to divide the moral realm of normative discourse from nonmoral realms. One can do this without going on to make normative judgments of the moral kind oneself, as a so-called amoralist would or as a social scientist *qua* social scientist should. That is, one can accept a certain definition of morality without thereby subscribing to any morality. On the other hand, of course, one can *both* accept a certain definition of morality *and* then enter the moral arena oneself, using moral considerations of the kind defined as a basis for evaluative judgments. Taking the MPV entails doing the second sort of thing, not just the first.

Now, I could at this point simply define taking the MPV as doing the second sort of thing more or less consciously. I am inclined to believe, however, that, behind any such acceptance of a certain sort of fact as relevant to one's judgments of persons, there must be some "principle of morals" in Hume's sense, i.e., something that moves us to approve or disapprove of persons, including ourselves and our own actions, on the grounds indicated—or something that constitutes the answer to what I earlier called the third metamoral project; and I therefore want to identify this, whatever it is, with the MPV or at least to make it central to taking the MPV. Just here, with a reference to Feinberg, Taylor introduces the attitude of equal respect for persons as a "pre-condition" of taking the MPV. I have objected to including equalitarianism as part of the essense of the MPV, even though I cannot but accept it as a moral principle when I myself take the MPV; but otherwise Taylor—and Baier too in his article—seem to me to be on the right track. Only I want now to equate taking the MPV with whatever it is that is what Taylor calls its "pre-condition"; i.e., I propose to equate taking the MPV not so much with the posture of accepting and using a certain sort of fact as reasons for judgments of goodness, rightness, and so forth (in the case of persons), as with that which generates or is the "source" in Bergson's sense of our adopting that posture. And I agree that this source is something nonegoistic and moving.

What then is the MPV, in my sense? Hume argued that it was "sympathy" or "the sentiment of humanity," and some Christians would say that it was *agape*. Bergson held that it is two things, depending on whether the morality it issues in is "open" or "closed." Somewhat similarly, Schopenhauer earlier maintained that "the foundation of morality" as it exists in the West is a partial but incomplete grasp of what is real behind the "veil of Maya." My own view is that the MPV is more neutral than benevolence, love, or sympathy—that it is just a Caring or Non-Indifference about what happens to persons and conscious sentient beings *as such,* of the kind that goes with the imaginative realization of their lives of which Royce and James wrote so eloquently, and which might take the form of sheer hate or malevolence—if this is possible for human beings, which I doubt.

I cannot refrain from quoting Agatha Christie here, as I often did in my classes—and I don't think I am going from the sublime to the ridiculous. In *The Mirror Crack'd* she has wise old Miss Marple describe the murdered person by comparing her with an Alison Wilde she once knew:

> [Alison Wilde] didn't know what people were like. She'd never thought about them. . . . It really comes from being self-centered and I don't mean selfish by that. . . . You can be kind and unselfish and even thoughtful. But if you're like Alison Wilde, you never really know what you may be doing.
>
> . . . Alison Wilde never thought of anybody else but herself. . . . She was the sort of person who tells you what they've done and what they've seen and what they've felt and what they've heard. They never mention what any other people said or did. Life is a kind of one-way track—just their own progress through it. Other people seem to them just like—like wallpaper in a room. . . . I think Heather Badcock was that kind of a person.
>
> . . . People like [her] . . . lack . . . any real consideration for the way their actions may affect other people. She thought always of what an action meant to *her,* never sparing a thought to what it might mean to somebody else.

The MPV is something Alison Wilde and Heather Badcock did not have.

Of course, this PV is not always consciously taken in ordinary moral discourse or thinking; perhaps it is not even taken in every culture that has a morality in my sense; my suggestion is only that it is directly or indirectly implicit in our selection of the kinds of reasons we regard as appropriate to the making of moral judgments proper. In this sense, this PV is what is behind morality, and hence is the MPV.

Unlike Baier and Taylor, I do not define the MPV by reference to the acceptance or use of any particular test of justifiability, validity, or truth, though I agree with them (and
Gewirth) that in making moral judgments, general or particular, we do and should claim that they are justifiable, if not
true or valid. Perhaps doing this is part of taking the MPV. On
the contrary, I propose to state the test of justifiability in terms
of the MPV, thus asserting thesis C in its natural sense, if not B.
A judgment that is moral by the criteria roughly described a few
moments ago is also justified if and only if it is a judgment that
would be agreed to by all who genuinely take the MPV and are
clear, logical, and fully knowledgeable about relevant kinds of
facts (empirical, metaphysical, or whatever).

6

There are problems for the MPVT just sketched, of course,
and I shall end by saying a little about some of them. (1) Like
Baier and Taylor, I hold that, in making a moral judgment,
particular or general, we are *claiming* that it or the principle behind it, or both, is justifiable in an intersubjective sense. I also
wish myself, when making a firsthand moral judgment, to claim
that it *is* justifiable in such a sense. Now, it is characteristic of
emotive and noncognitive meta-ethical theories to omit or
disown the making of such claims for moral judgments. Stevenson, in his retrospective postscript, insisted that it is linguistically proper to say of ethical judgments that they are true or
false, but in doing so he was not ascribing to them any kind of
intersubjective justifiability or unjustifiability. Am I then a cog-
nitivist or not? I have usually regarded myself as a noncogniti-
vist of a rather special sort; this is because I am reluctant to
think of evaluative or normative judgments as truly or falsely
ascribing properties to persons, actions, and so forth, or as following validly by the canons of logic from factual ones. I do,
however, want to insist that a full taking of the MPV involves
having a certain vivid imaginative insight of a broadly factual
sort into the lives of people and other sentient beings and that,
when we go on to formulate an ethical judgment, general or
particular, we are not just "emoting" from the MPV and "invit-
ing-so-to-speak" others to do likewise. We are in some sense
claiming that our judgment will be agreed to by all who take the
MPV and are clear-headed, logical, and fully and imaginatively
knowledgeable.

(2) The next question is whether any such claim is true. Will all those who take the MPV agree about basic moral judgments, particular or general? Nonmethodological relativists say no. I wish to say yes. But I do not mean to hold that those who take the MPV will *necessarily* agree, and, of course, I have no way of proving that they will *in fact* agree. On the other hand, the relativist, by the same token, has no way of proving, e.g., by the use of anthropological evidence, that they will not agree. Under these circumstances I elect to take their agreeing as an article of faith, though there is more to be said on both sides. Should it turn out that people who take the MPV do or would still disagree about basic ethical judgments, one can say that both of their conclusions are justifiable in a somewhat more relativized sense than mine—though not plausibly that both are true—but one must give up claiming that any conclusion is justifiable in the intersubjective way indicated in (1). The question here simply is one that a MPVT like mine cannot answer with certainty, as Gewirth pointed out. In this sense, my MPVT *must* remain at best a second-best.

(3) There is another way in which it may remain a second-best. Even if a MPVT like mine can establish one moral principle or value system as justifiable from the MPV and conflicting ones as not, it still would not thereby show that it is irrational not to be moral or not to live by that principle or value-system. It would still have done something significant, because it would have established a basis for answering questions about what is *morally* right or good, but it would not have given us an answer to the question of what we finally should do. To answer this question it must show that being moral by its standards is the rational way to live. Only if it can show this can it be better than second-best, *if* any such attempt as Gewirth's should succeed. But, as I said before, one must not assume that it cannot show this; and if it can, can Gewirth, Kant, or Spinoza do better?

(4) But now I must face the twofold question: (a) Why should one, i.e., is it rational to, take the MPV? (b) Why should one, i.e., is it rational to, be moral? These are, as Taylor pointed out, distinct questions. Roughly, (a) asks whether it is rational to be moral as versus nonmoral, and (b) whether it is rational to be moral as versus immoral. Here I follow Taylor in understanding the question how it is rational to live as the question how one would choose to live if one were free, clear-headed, logical, and had a vivid imaginative and complete knowledge of oneself and

the world. Taking the questions in this way, I must now admit
that neither I nor any other MPV theorist can show that being
moral in either sense is actually part of the rational life. There is
no way of proving at any point in time that one would choose to
be moral if . . . However, there is also no way of proving that
anyone would not; and so once again I am led to a postulate—in
this case, that we are all so constituted that we would choose
the moral life if . . .

(5) I come finally to the problem that has been plaguing me
most (in connection with my particular kind of MPVT), and I
can only try to state it, for I am not sure I have a solution. I have
suggested that taking the MPV is or includes a kind of direct
Caring about or Non-Indifference to what goes on in the lives of
people and consciously sentient beings as such, including others
besides oneself. Actually, it includes more, for it includes also
making evaluative or normative judgments, pure or hybrid,
about persons, actions, and so forth, on the basis of facts about
how they do or propose to affect the lives of such beings as such.
This means that it includes a concern for being rational in one's
judgments and perhaps in one's conduct too, for, whatever
Hume thought, the making of such judgments entails a commitment to reason, as Kant saw. My problem is this. I can conceive of someone, whom we may call Loverperson, who simply
loves people, animals, and so forth, without any thought of
having duties toward them or of their having rights; in Kant's
terms his or her love is purely "pathological," not "practical."
Now Loverperson need not make any evaluative or normative
judgments, but may do so—e.g., on harming someone by an act
done out of love he or she may say, "Oh, oh! That wasn't good"
or "That was the wrong thing to do." Loverperson is then
Caring and is making evaluative or normative judgments on the
basis of facts of the sort specified in my definition of the MPV. Is
Loverperson then taking the MPV and making moral judgments? Like Kant, I want to say no. But why isn't Loverperson
taking the MPV? The natural thing to say is that his or her
evaluative judgments are instrumental or in Kant's sense hypothetical; they say only what one should or should not do,
given that one loves, even if they are "assertoric" in form. *If* this
is the answer to my question, then I have only to say that taking
the MPV entails making evaluative judgments that are categorical or nonhypothetical, as I have already in effect maintained. That is, I must hold that taking the MPV includes

Caring and not only making normative judgments, but making nonhypothetical ones in the way indicated earlier. Does this do the job? I am not sure.[42]

And what if Loverperson insists that his or her judgments are meant to be nonhypothetical, saying what one should or should not do whether one is loving or not? Then his or her judgments would involve a concern for a kind of categorical rationality of judgment and action, *as well as* love of others. Should one say that *such* a Loverperson is taking the MPV and has a morality? Perhaps. It still remains true, however, that a Loverperson is not necessarily taking the MPV or having a morality, even though that person is Caring and using normative language. It is also true, I believe, that Caring need not take the form of love even when it does not take that of hate or malevolence either. It may simply take the more Kantian form of *respect* for persons (or conscious sentient beings). Then it would be somewhat different from love. One might describe it as the attitude of attributing "intrinsic worth" to persons (or conscious sentient beings), as Taylor does; but, if I was right in what I said earlier, this would simply be the attitude of seeing persons (and conscious sentient beings) as having duties and rights, or both, as such or non-hypothetically. Perhaps one should say, then, that the MPV may take two forms: (a) the Stoic-Kantian form just described, and (b) the more Christian form of the Loverperson who sees his or her Oughts as nonhypothetical.

(6) A critic like Anscombe or Foot may ask how the Caring person comes by the concept of a nonhypothetical Ought and what validity that concept has. I shall not try to answer such questions now, though I would if I could.[43]

APPENDIX

Perhaps one should distinguish two contexts of moral judgment and discourse in a different way than does Taylor—in fact, in something like Baier's way (in his article). (1) There is the context provided by what Locke called "the law of opinion or reputation" and H. L. A. Hart "positive social morality." Here one makes moral judgments, particular or general, from within the social moral code one has in some sense taken over; in Riesman's terms one is here either tradition-directed or inner-directed, but not really or at least not necessarily autonomous. In

his article Baier regarded this as the first stage of moral deliberation and judgment, but, as we saw, it is not or need not always
be. It comes closer to being the first stage in anyone's moral
development, though it may and perhaps even should be one of
the contexts in which we operate at any stage, as I understand
Hare to have been arguing recently. For many people it is, no
doubt, the only context of moral judgment. But (2) there is also
the context of a more autonomous morality to which one may
come, a morality which is in some sense really independent, and
possibly even critical, of prevailing positive morality— something
nonpositive such as Socrates was trying to foster. Both Taylor's
contexts, as he thinks of them, fall within this second kind of
morality, as does Baier's second stage of moral deliberation.

Using these terms, I think that what I have been talking about
is the business of taking the MPV in morality of the second
kind—as did Taylor and (in his book) Baier. However, I would
want to maintain—and did in effect maintain in my paper—that
the prevailing positive code of a society is a moral, as versus a
nonmoral one, if and only if it in some sense embodies the MPV
as I have described it, though perhaps only implicitly or uncon-
sciously. Thus I would hold that my MPVT also gives an account in some sense of whatever reasoning there has been behind any positive code that is a moral one. In any case, of
course, I would insist that it describes the reasoning that is or
should be behind any moral criticism of such a positive code or
of any other social institution (law, education, and so forth).

FOOTNOTES

1. See Alan Gewirth, *Reason and Morality* (Chicago: Univ. of
Chicago Press, 1978), ch. 1; but also his "Moral Rationality,"
reprinted in J. Bricke (ed.), *Freedom and Morality* (Lawrence:
Univ. of Kansas, 1976).

2. Josiah Royce, *The Religious Aspect of Philosophy* (Boston:
Houghton Mifflin and Co., 1885), pp. 146–162; William James,
On Some of Life's Ideals (New York: Henry Holt and Co., 1899).

3. Kurt Baier, "The Point of View of Morality," *Australasian
Journal of Philosophy* XXXII (1954).

4. J. M. Brennan, *The Open Texture of Moral Concepts* (New York: Barnes and Noble, 1977), p. 19.

5. P. W. Taylor, "On Taking the Moral Point of View," *Midwest Studies in Philosophy*, III (1978), p. 52.

6. See, e.g., Taylor, *Normative Discourse* (Englewood Cliffs, N.J.: Prentice-Hall Inc., 1961), ch. 12.

7. R. B. Brandt, *Ethical Theory* (Englewood Cliffs, N.J.: Prentice-Hall Inc., 1959), p. 275.

8. See R. M. Hare, *Freedom and Reason* (Oxford: Clarendon Press, 1963), pp. 37, 164, 216ff; *Applications of Moral Philosophy* (Berkeley and Los Angeles: Univ. of California Press, 1972), pp. 58-60.

9. For reference see note 3. The quotations below are from pp. 108, 123.

10. *The Moral Point of View* (New York: Random House, 1965), p. 92. My references are all to this revised edition of his book.

11. P. 92.

12. Pp. 90f.

13. P. 91.

14. P. 95.

15. See p. 91 and ch. 7.

16. P. 155.

17. See notes 5 and 6.

18. Cf. pp. 144, 155, 296, 317, 319.

19. Pp. 111ff.

20. Pp. 115f.

21. P. 123.

22. Pp. 121f.

23. See J. C. Thornton, "Can the Moral Point of View be Justified?" as reprinted in *Readings in Contemporary Ethical Theory* (Englewood Cliffs, N.J.: Prentice Hall Inc., edited by K. Pahel and M. Schiller, 1970), p. 452.

24. See note 5.

25. Taylor levels this charge against Baier in "The Ethnocentric Fallacy," *Monist* 47 (1963). Kai Nielsen's reply is in "On Moral Truth" in *Studies in Moral Philosophy* (Oxford: Basil Blackwell, 1968), pp. 14–18.

26. Pp. 36f.

27. Op. cit. in note 25, pp. 568–570.

28. Pp. 44f (my italics).

29. P. 38.

30. P. 37.

31. P. 56.

32. "Moral Rationality" as cited in note 1, p. 116.

33. *Reason and Morality*, p. 21.

34. Ibid, p. 1.

35. See, e.g., "The Concept of Morality" in K. E. Goodpaster (ed.), *Perspectives on Morality* (Notre Dame: Univ. of Notre Dame Press, 1976), p. 126; also the item cited below in note 42, pp. 111ff.

36. P. 4.

37. Pp. 9-11.

38. Pp. 20-21.

39. P. 1.

40. Op. cit., p. 45.

41. Here see the paper cited in note 35, but also the one with the same title (written earlier) reprinted in G. Wallace and A. D. M. Walker, *The Definition of Morality* (London: Methuen & Co., Ltd., 1970), pp. 169f; Taylor, pp. 315ff; G. J. Warnock, *Contemporary Moral Philosophy* (London: Macmillan, 1967), p. 54; A. Quinton, "The Bounds of Morality" in H. E. Kiefer and M. K. Munitz (eds.), *Ethics and Social Justice* (Albany: State Univ. of New York Press, 1970), pp. 127f.

42. I wrestle with this problem in "Three Questions about Morality," *Monist* 63 (1980), pp. 14–17, 115–117.

43. But see the work just cited, pp. 40–44.

PROBLEMS OF CONTEMPORARY UTILITARIANISM: REAL AND ALLEGED

R. B. Brandt

Everybody believes that some actions, or types of action, are morally wrong, in some sense or other; or, in different terminology, that certain types of action are ones it is a person's moral duty or obligation to do or to avoid doing. Many philosophers, however, have wanted to introduce some order into this chaos of opinions about what is morally wrong. They have sought to find a small number of fundamental principles of right and wrong—fundamental in the sense both that they are justified principles, and ones from which all justified beliefs about which actions are wrong can be deduced logically, given the aid of some lemmas about matters of fact such as what will be the consequences of a certain kind of act. A few philosophers have thought that there is only one such fundamental principle. One of these principles is the theory of Immanuel Kant, otherwise known as his famous "categorical imperative"; another, perhaps, is a recent one of John Rawls. The oldest of these, one which has shown vitality and appeal for philosophers literally over thousands of years, is utilitarianism, the view that the benefit or harm done by an act, or class of actions, or something of the sort, fixes whether an act is right or wrong morally. The term "utilitarianism" calls attention to the fact that it is good or harm done by some action or practice or trait of character that makes it right or wrong morally; the thought is that if actions did not have good or bad consequences there would be no point in morality, or in talk of right and wrong. If acts of incest or homosexual contact or deceit are wrong, it is because the acts or practice or traits of character have impact for good or ill, happiness or unhappiness.

Unfortunately from the point of view of simplicity, there are various different kinds of utilitarianism. One of them, which seems to have been thought of only in the past century, is called "act-utilitarianism"; the thesis is that a particular act is right if and only if there is no other act the agent could perform at the time which would have, or would probably have (on the agent's evidence) better consequences. Such important persons as G. E.

Moore, Henry Sidgwick, and Bertrand Russell advocated this view about the turn of the present century. A second form, which is much older and probably more influential among philosophers at present, is called "rule-utilitarianism"; its thesis is roughly that an act is morally right if and only if roughly the prevalence of a moral code (or structure of character) permitting that act would be as beneficial as an otherwise similar moral code which prohibited it. There are other types of utilitarianism, but these two seem the most important at the present time.

Contemporary critics of utilitarianism, who are incidentally quite numerous (a recent critical article in the *Yale Law Review* anticipated the demise of utilitarianism by speculating that a half-dozen adherents today are all that separates utilitarianism from extinction!), generally center their fire on the *first* form of the theory. Unfortunately it is then often implied, if not said, that criticism of the first form disposes of utilitarianism in all its forms. That is a mistake. Adherents of rule-utilitarianism are themselves quite critical of act-utilitarianism, although the theories are fairly closely related. (Some act-utilitarians think we should teach our children, and ourselves, rule-utilitarianism, along with some background qualifications.)

In what follows I shall ignore the first form and its problems, since there is not space to discuss both forms, and since the second form seems to me much the more plausible. The choice is not eccentric, I think, despite the number of thoughtful advocates today of act-utilitarianism; I believe *most* philosophers who advocate utilitarianism in some form today are in the rule-utilitarian camp. Another reason for concentrating on rule-utilitarianism is that some of its problems have not received comparable notice.

1. What Is Rule-utilitarianism?

Rule-utilitarianism is the older form of utilitarianism. One can argue that it goes back to Epicurus (341–270 B.C.), who was a utilitarian about laws. He said that "natural justice is a symbol or expression of expedience" and that "among the things accounted just by conventional law, whatever in the needs of mutual intercourse is attested to be expedient, is thereby stamped as just . . . "[1] One might also argue that the theory of natural law held by St. Thomas is utilitarian. However that may be, rule-utilitarianism as a theory of right *action*—not of right laws—goes back at least as far as Richard Cumberland in 1672. Bishop Berkeley, in his *Passive Obedience* (1712), was the first to distinguish clearly between the two forms of utilitarianism, and he opted for the second form. More specifically, he asserted that what we are morally bound to do is *not* to do whatever we believe will produce most good or happiness, but to follow certain moral laws, prohibiting or enjoining certain *types* of action —these being God's laws as identified by revelation or natural reason—and that these laws have been selected by God because, in his benevolence, he wants the happiness of mankind and knows that following these laws will maximize it. God incidentally also lets it be known that it will not be to the long-range interest of anyone to infringe his laws; so the theory provides motivation to do what is right. Now, if you delete the part about God in Berkeley's view, you have the skeleton of much the kind of rule-utilitarianism I wish to discuss. It was roughly held by J. S. Mill. We of course have to flesh out the account a bit.

The first thing we have to do, in order to get the idea, is to think of the *morality* of a society: that is, of people in the society mostly sharing certain aversions or desires (partly as a matter of innate or learned benevolence, but partly as a result of a process of motivational learning we need not try to specify) to certain act-types, as such. These act-types presumably will include aversions to hurting others, telling lies, and breaking promises. But there are not only aversions: there are also learned dispositions to experience guilt-feelings in case a person does act contrary to these aversions, and there is disapproval of others when *they* act contrary. There is also admiration of others who do what we'd like to have them do even when we wouldn't disapprove of them if they didn't—for instance, if they do what we say is going over and beyond the call of duty. Further, we disapprove, and are aversive to, various kinds of acts in *different degrees*; we would not commit murder and we disapprove intensely of anyone who does (without excuse), but we also don't like it very well when a person brushes off a request for a match, but in the latter case the disapproval is slight, and we ourselves feel only a slight aversion to doing that ourselves. Consciences are also equipped with a system of excuses, in the sense that conscience is so formed that we don't feel guilty, or at least don't disapprove of others, if the infractions of the primary aversions arise from certain inabilities, say ignorance of fact, insanity, a state of extreme fear, and so on.

You may not like this *motivational* description of what conscience is, but I think you will find most of it in Mill's third chapter, and to some extent in the fifth chapter, of *Utilitarianism*. At any rate, to my mind that *is* what conscience is, and the morality of a society is nothing more than the total fact of the consciences of the members of the society; or, if you like, you can say that the "morality" of the society is the conscience of the average man, or something like that.

If this is what a morality—or moral code—is, then how shall we define a "rule-utilitarian"? As a first approximation let us say that he thinks that *right actions* are ones of a type permitted by the moral code *optimal* for the society of the agent, and that an optimal code is one the total cost-benefit impact of the prevalence of which (including the teaching of and living with the type of conscience in question) is to maximize welfare or what is good (so, utility). This explanation leaves open the possibility that a particular right act by itself may not maximize benefit.

This definition does not imply anything about what a utilitarian *means* by "right" or "optimal," or about how a utilitarian will *justify* the main thesis. He may mean by an act's being "right" its being one of which an informed impartial and normal person would not disapprove, or its being one permitted by a moral code which would be supported by any rational fully informed person (or one fully informed except for facts which would make it impossible to be impartial); or he may think that we all understand "right" perfectly well but that the concept is too basic to admit of a definition. And he may *justify* his thesis by arguing that it describes the moral code an informed impartial person would support; or he may say that his principle jibes with his own moral intuitions or what he takes to be the deep moral intuitions of common sense. But a person can be a utilitarian without doing either of these things: without having any particular account of the meaning of "right" or "optimal," and without offering any substantial justification of his thesis; he can simply *advocate* the utilitarian principle. So I shall *define* a "rule-utilitarian" as a person who thinks that what is right or wrong morally is identified by the content of an "optimal" moral code for the agent's society.

On the rule-utilitarian view, then, to find what is morally right or wrong we need to find which actions would be permitted by a moral system for the agent's society—"optimal" in the sense explained. This conception, however, raises a question—the first one I wish to mention as something a rule-utilitarian has a "problem" about. For an agent's society will comprise various subgroups, and it could be that the moral code optimal for one is not quite identical with the moral code optimal for another. For instance, perhaps the moral code comprising the consciences of physicians and lawyers should at least be more articulated in certain areas than that of the general public. There is no reason to burden the general public with, say, aversion to refusing to treat patients who cannot pay, or to breaching a relation of confidentiality. Remember that we have to include the learning-costs in a cost-benefit analysis of a moral system, just as in the case of a system of criminal justice we have to count the costs of enforcement as well as the benefits of conformity, in deciding which system is the best. If we bear this in mind, then the possibility must confront us that perhaps the rule-utilitarian must recognize special moralities for such persons as physicians who, unlike the general public, meet certain problems regularly and need to have an intuitive response not requiring long inference from general principles. Similarly, the possibility must occur to us that possibly the morality optimal for children is not necessarily the morality optimal for adults. Rule-utilitarians, then, may be free to think that the justified moral code for physicians, lawyers, children, bishops, and university students will differ. The identification of such possible special codes is part of the subject-matter of "professional ethics."

This conception poses a question I shall be content merely to raise, without trying to answer it: Could the optimal moral code for a physician or a politician or an officer in the military direct him to do something incompatible with what the optimal code for the general public would prescribe for the same situation? Presumably we *do* think that the optimal code for one *society* might lead to behavior incompatible with that to which the optimal code for another society might lead. If that situation is possible, there is the further problem of what is the really right thing to do when these codes conflict. A related problem, for a rule-utilitarian who thinks that the actions of *governments* may be morally right or wrong, is: Must we talk of an "optimal moral code" for governments? Can we think of governments as quasi-persons, and talk of an optimal conscience for them? Or may we talk, not of the acts of *governments* being right or wrong, but only of the morally right or wrong acts of office-holders, or politicians? Rule-utilitarians should think more about this.

There is another complication which I shall only pause to mention. Suppose that a *law*—but we might generalize to *any institution*—is less than optimal, by the utilitarian standard. Might it still be *morally* acceptable? Or suppose it is optimal. Is it then necessarily also morally acceptable? We know that such writers as Rawls would say No to both these questions; there is no necessary correlation between optimality and moral acceptability. But what may the rule-utilitarian say? He *might* take either option. First, he might just identify the moral acceptability of an institution, say a law, with its optimality, in the context of other institutions in the society. But he can also deny this, and say that what makes an institution morally acceptable is not *its* optimality, but whether an optimal *moral code* would require persons to work to change it, or work to preserve it. So a utilitarian could say that the tax law, or welfare system, might be optimal, but conceivably not morally acceptable because perhaps morality requires more equality. So the utilitarian might say that the optimality of the moral code is the optimality relevant to the moral acceptability of an institution, not the optimality of the institution itself. Very likely, of course, there will normally be a close connection between the two.

One might ask: How should a utilitarian decide which of these lines to take? I propose not to try to answer this question,[2] but I shall shortly consider how the rule-utilitarian must go about resolving such difficulties.

2. What Is Utility?

The rule-utilitarian, then, says that right action is action permitted by the moral code for the agent's society that would be optimal, net-*benefit* maximizing, *utility*-maximizing. But what is meant to count as benefit or utility? One traditional answer has been: pleasure, or hedonic tone, positive or negative—or happiness, which may be construed as the same thing. Now many philosophers have thought *this* is not what we should try to maximize, and one is taking only a crude view of human nature if one thinks it is. What then should we add? J. L. Mackie suggests: "liberty of thought and discussion, thought and discussion themselves, understanding of all sorts of things, including ourselves and other human beings, a self-reliant, enterprising, and experimental spirit and way of life, artistic creation and craftsmanship of many sorts, the enjoyment and appreciation of beauty, and general participatory self-government both in smaller institutions and in the determination of large scale social policies and laws."[3] He says this in criticism of utilitarianism of all kinds. How much of a criticism is this? Is utilitarianism in all its forms too narrow because it is committed to a hopelessly narrow view of what is good?

The first thing to note is that there is no *logical* connection between the various types of utilitarianism and hedonism, and none between a deontological ethics and nonhedonism. It is true that the utilitarian says we are to identify right action by appeal to *maximizing* net-benefit or utility, but he leaves open *what* that is. One can say: one is to maximize what is intrinsically good, and go on to say, as such "ideal utilitarians" as Moore and Rashdall did, that various states of affairs besides pleasure are intrinsically good—say, knowledge, virtue, friendship. One could then say, as these ideal utilitarians did, that the right action is fixed by the maximization of the intrinsically good, and then to propose that one can make comparative judgments about the intrinsic worth of knowledge and virtue (and the like) so that one can determine, roughly, when the good is being maximized.

There is, however, a good reason for avoiding this multiplication of intrinsic goods, if it is possible—for different persons, with different intuitions about how intrinsically good some of these things are, may come out in very different places in their estimates of the total goodness that one action, or moral code, is likely to produce, as compared with another. So philosophers have wanted to find a view, I think, which avoids so much reliance on intuitions. This is one consideration that attracts toward hedonism, for the hedonist holds that only one sort of thing is good in itself; so the question of which code or action maximizes the good reduces to the factual question of how much enjoyment is produced. There is, however, another type of theory which also avoids reliance on intuitions, and which avoids the alleged narrowness of the hedonist view. This is the view that "utility" is to be defined not in terms of pleasure, but in terms of desire-satisfaction or interest-satisfaction. Thus, whereas the hedonist says a state of affairs X is better than a state of affairs Y if it contains more pleasure, the desire-satisfaction theory says X is better than Y if more people desire it, or, if we can quantify preferences, there is more preference for X over Y than for Y over X. This last sounds a bit complex, but many people think that numbers can be assigned to a person's desires, unique up to a linear transformation, by observation of betting behavior; then if the strengths of some among different persons' desires can be compared—or some other way found of aggregating preferences—then the interest-satisfaction theory provides a way to identify which policy or behavior would maximize utility as defined in terms of desire-satisfaction. Thus hedonism and the interest theory have emerged as leading contenders for a conception of utility suited for a simple maximizing theory of right and wrong conduct—that is, for one which is simple in the sense of holding that in a sense, only one sort of thing is good. Of the two theories, the second appears to be more popular at present, perhaps for one or more of three reasons. First, it allows that a wide variety of different states of affairs can be good—anything that can be wanted for itself. Second, it is thought easier to measure the strength of desires than to measure an amount of pleasure. Third, the desire theory may seem more democratic; it goes on the basis of what people in fact want, not on the basis of what will give them happiness—we are not to deny people what they want just because we think it will make them happier in the long-run.[4]

From a practical point of view, the two theories are not all that different, since desire and pleasure are closely related—for people want to be in pleasant states and avoid unpleasant ones, other things being equal. Further, other things being equal, getting what one wants is something pleasant and frustration unpleasant; so there is a close connection between desire and pleasure, but the implications of the two theories are not exactly identical.

I shall not attempt here to adjudicate between these theories, the desire and the pleasure theories of utility. But I do want to make three remarks.

The first is that the hedonistic theory must obviously make up its mind what pleasure is; misunderstanding of the meaning of pleasure can lead to faulty attitudes toward the theory. I think myself that what it is for some element of experience to be pleasant is just for it to be making the person, at the time, want to continue or repeat it, just for itself and not for extraneous reasons. This view has been called a "motivational" theory of pleasure. If we accept something like this, then our attention is called to the fact that it is not only physical sensations that are pleasant; a person can thoroughly enjoy reading a book, solving a crossword puzzle, or even writing a philosophy paper. This leads to my second point. Such critics as Mackie have thought that utilitarianism, in its hedonist form, is very narrow in its conclusions about what it is to be maximized, or is good. But when we start surveying the various other things philosophers have thought are good, such as knowledge, or friendship and love, or relationships of trust, or such qualities of character as courage or fair-mindedness, we need to ask ourselves whether all these do not make life more satisfying (pleasant in the explained sense), and whether we would be much interested in them if they didn't. The critic may reply by saying that of course all these things add to happiness, but that they would still be worthwhile in themselves even if they didn't add to happiness. Yet if the critic has to take this line his point is much harder to establish, and one is left feeling that the happiness theory is not so narrow after all.

Such critics' points are, of course, blunted altogether if we adopt the desire theory of utility, for then the utilitarian can say, of anything the antihedonist says is intrinsically good, that it is something people do desire and hence the utilitarian will think it is one of the things to be maximized.

I come now to my third comment: that there are some difficulties in the desire theory, to which I shall allude just in a sentence or two. First, I don't think we really want to maximize satisfaction of desire in general. People desire all sorts of things that it is idiotic to desire. I think we should want to maximize at most the satisfaction of those desires people *would* have if they were fully informed about everything which would tend to make them change their desires if they knew about it. Call this the "informed desire" theory. Even so, I doubt if we really want to maximize desire-satisfaction as such; I think mostly we are concerned to help people get what they want because we think it will make them happy to get it, or when not getting it will make them sad or frustrated. There is a further and complicated point, which I cannot develop. It is that people's *desires*—their utility functions if you like—are continually undergoing change. So one wonders which desires one is to try to satisfy at any time. Is it only the *unchanging* desires? Ones the person has now but won't have later? Ones that the person will have at the time he is to get what he wants? I find it very difficult to find any formulation that is convincing.

The utilitarian, then, does have to make up his mind what is his conception of the "utility," the maximizing of which is to be the test of right and wrong. This topic is one he ought to think more about. But the charge that the utilitarian is committed to a crude or narrow view of what is good seems manifestly mistaken.

3. Figuring Maximization: Do We Just Add Up All the Utilities?

For the sake of simplicity let us assume from here on that we are opting for a hedonist conception of "utility." Let us think of pleasure as being measurable, so that the basic units are *hedon-moments*, where a "hedon-moment" is an experience, for one minute, with a pleasure level of plus-one. We shall speak of these as sometimes having a negative value when the pleasure level is negative. An experience for one minute with a hedonic tone of level plus-two would be two hedon-moments, just as an experience for two minutes with a hedonic tone of level plus-one—and so on.

Given these concepts, we might then say that moral system *A* is more utility-productive than moral system *B* if and only if the net balance of hedon-moments from getting *A* current in the society and keeping it there would be, or would probably be, greater than the net balance from getting *B* into place and keeping it there. When a system *A* is more optimal in this sense than any other system, we can say that *A* is the optimal moral system, and that its content fixes which acts are morally right or wrong.

There are some apparent implications of this formulation, however, which lead one to wonder whether it is exactly correct, and to wonder, in case changes are called for, what might be the justification for making changes. I shall consider three sets of implications, possibly not unrelated.

The first set of these comprises implications about the morality of population control. The implications have excited mostly act-utilitarians, and in fact to my knowledge they have not been discussed carefully by any rule-utilitarian. Some of the worrisome implications, or possible implications (when we think it out they may *not* be implications for the rule-utilitarian) are these: (1) We might increase the total net balance of hedon-moments either by making existing people happier, or by producing more people who are predictably happy. Indeed, it is conceivable that we could maximize net happiness more easily by producing many babies, even at the cost of severe reduction in the standard of living of those who would otherwise have existed. Should we say, then, that it is morally obligatory to produce maximal hedon-moments by whatever manner? It would seem strange to answer affirmatively, but does not rule-utilitarianism as stated imply this? (2) A parent might have an obligation to sacrifice himself for an existing child, but we would ordinarily hardly think he need sacrifice himself for the sake of producing greater happiness by producing a child. Why not, if more hedon-moments would be produced by this policy? (3) We tend to think it is obligatory (say, after information from amniocentesis) not to have an unhappy (defective) child, but feel no obligation to produce a child because we think it would be very happy. (Yet, we think it justified to produce a great many children, even when the probability is high that some of them will be defective; so the happiness of many seems to discharge from the obligation not to produce some few who will probably be wretched.) But the conception of maximizing net hedon-moments seems not to allow for this distinction. Is the above formulation overly simple? Or do these problems, which do worry act-utilitarians, somehow not arise on the rule-utilitarian theory?

It has been suggested that the theory ought to say that the optimal moral code is the one that promises to maximize the *average* net balance of hedon-moments, not the total net balance; but recent discussion has shown that this change would not bring the theory more nearly into conformity with intuitions—rather the opposite.

With some trepidation, I suggest that at least most of the consequences do *not* follow from the rule-utilitarian thesis as stated, although I concede that a good deal more discussion is warranted. To see this, we should ask ourselves what moral requirements about procreation would be included in an optimal moral code. One such rule probably would be to abort fetuses reliably predicted to issue in seriously defective (hence probably unhappy) infants, since the total impact is presumably negative (considering the prospective marginal happiness of their own lives and the huge cost to others). Now, should there also be a moral requirement to have a child if one thought, with good reason, that it would probably be quite happy and hence would be an addition to the happiness of the world? The benefit of such a moral rule seems highly dubious. How happiness-productive would it be for parents to feel bound to produce babies they don't want, for the sake of having more happiness in the world? It seems reasonable to expect the parents would not be very happy with having the child (research indicates they are not happy, normally, as things are, in the usual case); and it seems reasonable to expect that the unwanted child would have fewer than the normal chances for a happy life. There may be special exceptions: royal families with some obligation to continue the family line; patriotic persons in a militaristic country which requires young people as cannon-fodder; geniuses whose offspring may very well contribute enormously to the welfare of mankind. In proposing such a rule for the normal case, there is an additional problem having to do with difficulties in teaching any such rule. The most successful method of teaching moral rules is through showing how behavior of a certain sort leads to harm, to which the normally sympathetic person is already averse. But could such teaching succeed if the "harm" in question is only the loss of utility owing to the non-existence of a child which is not born? No one is being *injured* by merely failing to exist.

For much the same reason it seems that an optimal moral code would require a parent to sacrifice himself for the greater benefit of an existing child—or perhaps for the sake of an equal benefit to the child, indeed possibly a lesser benefit. But it could hardly require that parent to make a sacrifice in order to produce another child just because it would be happy (perhaps, however, for the happiness of the already-existing siblings).

Furthermore, it is quite evident that in the present state of the world, it is absurd to suppose that, as a general rule, one's best way of maximizing utility is by producing more people; given all the hunger in the world, it appears there are already too many people. So rule-utilitarianism will hardly advocate a moral rule requiring couples to procreate. Should it, however, advocate a conditional moral rule, for the situation in which more people really would add to the world's happiness? It would seem that we might well postpone trying to teach our children any such conditional moral rule until the time it might have some realistic utility! Unless the need for more people is very important, it would hardly be beneficial, for reasons already stated, to try to teach such a rule.

One might ask why a rule-utilitarian does not advocate a rule prohibiting all procreation, considering that *some* infants are going to be defective and presumably unhappy, if he does not think there is *some* obligation to produce happy infants. I think the rule-utilitarian will say this in reply: First, an optimal moral code will contain no rule requiring procreation, except for very special situations (e.g., royal couples). But it recognizes that, say, nine out of ten infants are normal and let us suppose will lead lives more happy than not. So there is a benefit in children being produced, by parents who want them. Hence, the misery of the tenth and defective child is not enough to outweigh the benefit of the nine healthy children. The benefits are enough, then, to render it morally permissible to have a child even when it is not known the child will be healthy and normal; this is consistent with it not being morally permissible to have a child which predictably will be defective and unhappy.

The rule-utilitarian theory, then, seems not to have embarrassing implications for this type of problem. In view of the heavy weather which writers on population control have made in this area, however, it seems a bit reckless for a rule-utilitarian to feel smug about the implications of his theory for this area of moral thinking. Nevertheless, I do not feel the rule-utilitarian need feel alarmed by some of the bizarre situations for which some writers seem to have firm intuitions contrary at least to the implications of some forms of act-utilitarianism, e.g., the case of a post-atomic-war world in which only two persons are left, who might—if it were thought to be morally obligatory— start off a new human race from test-tube babies they knew how to produce, but at considerable sacrifice of personal pleasure. Should the moral code contain a rule dealing with this situation? And *is* there a *moral* obligation to do one thing rather than another?

Let us turn now to a second set of implications which rule-utilitarianism, in my opinion, really does have, but which run counter to the intuitions of some writers.

I have explained rule-utilitarianism in such a way that hedon-moments, or units of utility, are counted equally, irrespective of who has them: rich or poor, animal or human being, existing human being or one who will exist a hundred years from now. But one might want to change the theory: to go in for heavy discounts of people who will exist only in the future, or for the pleasures of animals.

Now the consistent utilitarian will himself introduce some discounts, of a sort. For instance, if he is choosing between policy A which for certain will produce n-units of utility tomorrow, and policy B which has a three-to-one chance of producing n-units of utility a hundred years from now, he will, other things being equal, opt for policy A. As I have explained utilitarianism, this too is part of the definition: the optimal moral code is the one which maximizes net *expectable* utility. Similarly, if one is choosing between a moral code which equates highly probable human pleasure with pretty speculative animal pleasure, and a code which prefers the former, for the same reason the rule-utilitarian will go for the latter. (This is not at all to say that we do not know that the suffering of hogs, as currently raised for the market, is more important than the saving of a few pennies in cost to consumers!)

Some writers have wanted to discount the hedon-units of future human beings, and of present animals, much more than this. Numerous economists wish to discount the welfare of future generations, but for obscure reasons. (It has been argued that rational persons all do discount *their own* future satisfactions else, given current interest rates, they would put off consumption, as much as possible, to the distant future.) And even Mill argued, for equally obscure reasons for a hedonist, that it is better to have Socrates dissatisfied than a pig satisfied.

One might say that the problem here is not a problem about the definition of rule-utilitarianism, or a formulation of the theory of the relation between utilities and moral obligations, but just a problem about what is really good or "utile"; so it may be said that Mill and others didn't think pleasure itself to be really good unless it were the pleasure of a rational being; and similarly that pleasure (or being an object of desire) in the future is not really a good thing, but only pleasure now. Yet one need not say this. One might hold that pleasure is the one and only good, but still hold that only the good of rational beings generates obligations; and one might hold that being pleasant in the future and being pleasant now are equal goods, but pleasure now generates much more powerful obligations than prospective pleasures in the distant future.

But would anyone who held this latter view be a utilitarian? Isn't the utilitarian committed to treating all hedon-moments, or utiles, equally? If someone doesn't count the utilities of animals or future generations equally, would we want to call him a "utilitarian" at all? Such a person would certainly be a special kind of utilitarian, but he would look a great deal more like Sidgwick than he would look like W. D. Ross, Kant, or Rawls. He would still be saying that right and wrong are fixed by connection with utilities, but in a somewhat less simple fashion.

If one asks how a person could come to hold such a queer form of utilitarianism, the retort can be: What makes him hold some simpler form of utilitarianism? There is no self-contradiction in a person accepting an "ideal observer" theory of what "morally right" means, and espousing a utilitarianism in which the utilities of animals do not count—indeed one in which the utilities of male human beings do not count. Or suppose you say that moral principles are right only if they would be agreed to by self-interested rational human beings choosing behind a veil of ignorance. Why might not such beings, who *do* know they are *human*, ignore the utilities of animals in selecting a form of utilitarianism? Or, suppose you say that what is right is fixed by the moral system that a fully rational, informed, and rationally benevolent person would support for a society in which that person expected to live. Is there not at least a question whether the person would choose a utilitarian system which defined obligations in such a way as to discount the utilities of animals and future generations?

At any rate, this seems to me an issue about which rule-utilitarians should think more, although my own view is that no good reasons have been given for writing down the utility of animals, or of future generations, in determining moral obligations now.

Let us turn now to a third way of modifying the simple conception of how to count utilities—that is, that all be counted equally. The problem I wish to consider is one that has been posed by writers sometimes called "negative utilitarians." I propose to start with some intuitions on which these writers insist, and then work back to possible rule-utilitarian accommodations of these intuitions.

The intuitions on which these writers seem to insist are these: (1) There is an obligation to avoid doing what will on balance cause harm, that is, reduce utility levels below where they would have been had nothing been done; and this obligation is stronger than the obligation to do an equal amount of good, namely, to raise a utility level above where it would have been had nothing been done. (2) There is, however, an obligation to *reduce misery*—just no obligation to do what will raise the utility level of persons when, if nothing were done, their utility level would already be above the misery level. Briefly, you are not to harm, and you are to relieve misery; but there is no obligation otherwise to improve the state of sentient beings. There seems a certain conflict of these intuitions at one point: what if the only way you can relieve misery is through harming some who are better off? One implication of these intuitions also does not seem convincing: it is that there is no obligation to increase the well-being of those above the misery level, even very substantially, when this can be done at little or no cost to yourself.[5]

One modification of this general idea would be to contrast, not obligation versus no obligations, but only strong versus weak obligations. Then there would be a strong obligation to relieve misery, but only a weak one to help the well-off.

The question I now wish to raise is whether there is any way in which we could come out with these intuitions on the basis of the kind of rule-utilitarianism I have been suggesting. That is, if an act is morally required only if it would be required by a moral code the getting and holding in place of which would be utility-maximizing for society, could we conclude that some or all of these intuitions are correct? There seem to be two ways in which one might so argue, the first the more plausible, the second less plausible but more interesting.

The first way is this. One might argue that the rule against harm, and the rule requiring relief of misery, are both rules respect for which is highly important. Moreover, they are easier to apply than other possible rules, since it is relatively easier to tell when we are harming someone, and it seems somewhat easier to tell when we are relieving misery than when we are just improving someone's status at a higher level. Again, such rules are rather congenial to people, and so they are relatively easy to teach. So the cost is low, the benefit high. Perhaps practical reflections of this sort are enough to justify a utilitarian in thinking that the rules mentioned are the *strongest* of our obligations, if not the only ones.

There is, however, another strategy that is rather interesting. One might just *weight more heavily* a gain or loss of hedon-moments below the indifference level. One might count hedon-moments above that level just a bit, enough to justify prohibiting harming people but not enough to justify the trouble of trying to improve their lot—whereas in the case of hedon-moments in the misery range, what we do is important, and we should try both to improve and also not to make even worse off. *Why* might a person weight hedon-moments in the misery range more heavily than equal hedon-moments above the misery range? A utilitarian, of course, *could* do this consistently; he would still be deriving his moral rules from a cost-benefit analysis of having them in place and keeping them there, but would just be weighting certain impacts much more heavily than others. But why should he? Some persons might be moved to adopt this kind of utilitarianism on the ground that human *sympathy* is (possibly) more moved to alleviate misery than it is to produce an equal increment of benefit to the well-off. Thus it might be said that fully rational and informed people would be sympathetic enough to prefer a utilitarianism of that sort. I think myself that this idea is a mistake. If a person's own personal hedonic scale has identified an interval on the positive side as the same as an interval in the unpleasant area, he will not prefer a gain of one interval to a gain at the other, and there is no reason why anyone else should do so (or regard a calibrated gain for one person as different in moral weight from an identical gain for another at some other point on the hedonic scale). So sympathy is pathological if it does not recognize that a hedon-moment is a hedon-moment, wherever it is; all identical intervals are morally equally important, wherever they happen to fall, on the plus or negative side. But I agree there is room for difference of opinion and that the problem is worth more thought.

4. Special Problems for Rule-Utilitarians

I now take leave of in-house problems about which rule-utilitarians ought to think more, and turn to just plain *objections* which philosophers have raised against either rule-utilitarianism, or utilitarianism in any form. I shall begin with objections to the kind of rule-utilitarianism I have been explaining. These objections come either from act-utilitarians who want to show how uninviting is the rule-utilitarian competition, or from anti-utilitarians who want to show that rule-utilitarianism has such serious difficulties that it is no better than act-utilitarianism, and hence not a form of utilitarianism which is at all plausible.

I shall state three objections to rule-utilitarianism, all related. Together they may be viewed as variations on a charge of Utopianism.

In order to state and appraise these objections, I must expand a bit on the conception of an "optimal" moral code. This conception is not that of a set of rules optimal in the sense that it would do most good if everyone actually conformed with them, 100 percent. What is meant is something more complex than this. We must recall that we mean by "a moral code" a set of desires-aversions directed at certain act-types in themselves, and dispositions to feel guilty about disconforming with these desires-aversions, and to disapprove such disconformity on the part of others, when there is no excuse. Now these dispositions may vary both in intensity, and *in how widespread* they are, with some degree of intensity, in a given society. The more widespread and the more intense an aversion to a certain sort of behavior, presumably the less frequent the behavior is apt to be; but also, the more widespread and the more intense, the greater the cost of the rule, both of teaching it and keeping it in being, the burdensomeness of the rule on the individual, and so on. Now, when we talk of the "optimality" of a moral code, we have to bear in mind both the benefits of reduced objectionable behavior on account of the rule, and also the long-term cost. So the moral code optimal for a given society is that whole system, with a given degree of average intensity and spread among the population for each of its components, which comes out best in a careful cost-benefit analysis of this sort. Needless to say, the optimal moral code (like the law) will normally not produce 100 percent compliance with all its rules; that would be too costly. It may, in small homogeneous populations; for example, physical violence of any sort is unheard of on the Hopi reservation. But mostly not. At any rate, that is what I mean by an "optimal code," and the rule-utilitarian thought is that an act is prima facie obligatory if and only if and to the degree that an optimal code would build in some degree of moral aversiveness to not performing it.

Philosophers do not generally object to rule-utilitarianism on the ground that we can't roughly know, if we put our minds to it and get the cooperation of psychologists and others, what the optimal code would look like. The problem that philosophers press appears to arise rather from their assumption that the optimal code, in this sense, is not or may not everywhere be in place.

We need not dispute that the optimal moral code is not in place, in many communities. But if we come close to home and ask if it is in place on the campus of the University of Michigan, or on your campus, it is not so clear that there is a big gap between the optimal and the actual. One seldom feels a burning need to write letters urging moral reform. It is true that professors and students are apt to be less sympathetic to welfare spending and higher taxation for the rich than they ought to be. At least to that extent there is disparity between the actual and the optimal. Still, let us admit, for the sake of argument, that in many places the optimal moral code is not the actual one. Let us then look at the objections.

The first objection is that it would be harmful for some people to *live* according to the actually optimal code, in a society where the optimal code is not actual; for so doing would be, at least often, either pointless or injurious. And, it is said, it is especially incoherent for a utilitarian to advocate behaving in a counter-productive way; his basic thesis is that utility is the point of morality; but here the rule-utilitarian is advocating behavior, following utopian rules, which is or may be harmful. For instance, it is said that the *optimal* moral code might call for no one ever to carry a lethal weapon, whereas living by such a code would not be a good idea in a society where everyone else was a trigger-happy gun-carrying demon.

It seems to me there is an adequate reply to this objection—and it is that it has not been shown that such harmful requirements would ever appear in an *optimal* moral code. An optimal moral code would surely give directions, in the gun-carrying society, to be prepared to defend oneself and one's family—of course *defend* only. The rule might be: "Never carry a gun when that can be done at no personal risk; otherwise carry a gun but use it only in self-defense." (Of course, an actual moral code would rarely include injunctions as specific as this one; it might, however, if a rule were aimed at meeting a specific problem about which it would be inadvisable to expect people to draw inferences from more abstract principles.) An optimal moral code may not always provide for doing the very best possible thing in every situation, for morality is a blunt instrument, like the law. But there has not, to my mind, been proof that an optimal code would prescribe doing seriously harmful things, in societies where others do not subscribe to it. True, it might well tell one to keep a promise when few others were doing so, and this might do little immediate good; but at least it would be a step in the direction of building up a convention of promise-keeping.

The critic might admit, as well he should, that it could well be that a person would *not* normally act harmfully if he lived in conformity with an optimal moral code, even when *that* code is far from being in place. But, it might be said—and this is the second suggestion—it would cause more than a little chaos for people generally to be *advised* just to live in accordance with an optimal moral code, when nobody has yet decided precisely what it is and certainly the average man has *no* idea. Act-utilitarianism has often been criticized on the ground that it would be chaotic if every individual really thought he were morally obligated to do just what seems to him likely to have the best consequences; so, wouldn't it be even more chaotic if every individual really thought he were morally obligated to do just whatever seemed to him to be required by an optimal moral code? How much has any individual thought about the optimal moral code, and how nearly would any two individuals come to agreement about what it is? This question has doubtless been discussed less than it should be. And I am prepared to admit that an answer must be a bit speculative. It will also make a difference who is being advised, and how; it would be absurd merely to throw at a person the advice that he live by the moral code optimal for his society, with no explanation; surely we are allowed to think that a person might be advised to do this only after an explanation of the conception of a moral code, and the value of moral codes, and the point of living by an optimal one. Further, one might expect explanation how far the actual moral code may serve as a guide to the optimal one, and anticipate that intelligent persons will then be incrementalists in their moral thinking, not wild-eyed utopians. (If a person gets no such explanations, the chances are he will ignore the advice and go on subscribing to the moral principles he held in the first place.) We may expect that, if they stop to reflect, they will see that this or that provision in the traditional morality has outlived its function and be willing to forget it. And on the other hand presumably they will see that new problems—say of an organized metropolitan society rapidly using up natural resources —demand some novel features in the moral code. To say these things is, as just remarked, to speculate about what would happen if intelligent people became convinced that when some problem arose, they ought to think through what an optimal code would be like and then live by it. But I have not seen proof that the results of this would be disastrous.

A third objection has been raised. It has been said that whereas it might be *nice* for people to act in accordance with an optimal moral code when that code is not in place, still one cannot seriously claim that is their *moral obligation*. Some critics say it may be morally obligatory to do what will in fact do most good in an actual situation even when the conventional moral code doesn't call for that, and it may even be obligatory to act in accordance with an optimal moral code if there is good reason to think that so doing would seriously tend to usher the optimal code into the status of being conventional; but, it is said, just to live by an optimal moral code for no further reason cannot be said to be one's *moral obligation*. To this objection there are retorts that seem to me quite adequate. We may begin by asking what are supposed to be the ground rules for deciding that one does or doesn't really have a moral obligation to do something. Doubtless answering this question adequately would lead us way back to the theory of the meaning and justification of moral beliefs. But if, say, one has shown that what one is morally obligated to do is what an impartial, informed, otherwise normal person would demand of one morally, or what would be demanded by a moral system which rational, fully informed persons with a rational degree of benevolence would support in preference to other moral systems and to no system at all; and it is further shown that these conceptions lead to the conclusion that what is obligatory is to follow an optimal moral code—it is hard to see why one must then start over and do something else in order to show that it is really morally obligatory to do this thing. Furthermore, we do not think that a person has no obligation to be kind to suffering animals, or to prisoners in a prison camp in wartime, just because other people don't or one can't say that conventional morality demands it. Are moral reformers never correct when they martyr themselves, as they see it, in order to discharge their moral obligations? There are at least two concessions we must make. First, we must agree that if one lives according to a moral code that demands more of one than the traditional moral code, one is doing something that it would not be disgraceful not to do—assuming, as I do, that to act disgracefully is to fall a bit below the normal level. Second, I agree that the normal social sanctions for behaving morally are absent in case one is living up to a standard which conventional morality does not require; indeed, one may *incur* moral sanctions, sometimes, for living in accordance with an optimal code—for instance, if one insists on treating persons of another race as social equals in a place where that is frowned upon. So, some of the reasons we ordinarily have for acting morally will be absent in such a case. But one must also point out that some of the reasons we ordinarily have for acting morally will also be present. For one thing, as often has been pointed out, one of the reasons for acting morally is often or usually our own sympathy or benevolence; and it would appear that sympathy or benevolence will always, or virtually always, be engaged on behalf of an optimal moral code. For another, most of us have somehow acquired a desire to do what we consider the morally right thing for no further reason. And this motive is going to be engaged on behalf of acting according to the provisions of an optimal code, if we are convinced that we ought morally to conform our conduct to those provisions. When all these considerations are taken into account, the claim that we have no moral obligation to live according to what we think is the optimal code, or according to what we think we ought to do, even when that code or standard is not in place in our society, seems to evaporate as a serious charge.

5. Economic Equality and the Justice of the Criminal Law

Thus far I have said nothing about two rocks upon which many philosophers think utilitarianism in all its forms must necessarily founder: the moral demand for economic justice or equality, and the moral requirement for legal punishment only where and to the extent it is deserved. Philosophical critics of utilitarianism suppose that there are here certain moral injunctions about both distributive and retributive justice which are well founded, and that these are inconsistent with the implications of utilitarianism in all its forms.

Space does not permit an extended discussion of these charges. I shall in fact limit my comments to the first, which strikes me as the more serious; but what I say about the first could be in principle transposed to a discussion about the second so that this limitation in any event will not be a loss. We need not, however, feel that only a lengthy discussion could possibly provide any kind of serious answer to these charges. For in this instance the critiques of utilitarianism are normally unsympathetic to an extent that borders on the ludicrous or at least the seriously unfair. The critics never work out carefully what a utilitarian theory implies for these topics; and when the critics identify the supposedly conflicting intuitive moral principles they often or always produce ones that are in fact highly dubious.

Let me spell this out briefly. If we look at present legislation regarding the welfare of the poor or underprivileged in the United States, we find aid to dependent children (in process of extension to childless couples and single persons), the food stamp program, a limited program of negative income tax, a medicaid program to take care of the health of those who are less well off, and an assistance program for the aged, the blind, and the disabled. How is all this paid for? Mostly out of general funds: from a progressive income tax levied on those who are more well off. Now I do not suggest that this system is perfect; far from it. But every one of the provisions of the system—which after all is a system for the redistribution of income—can be defended on utilitarian grounds. The utilitarian justification for all this is that a dollar taken in taxes from the wealthy would have done the wealthy far less good than the same dollar spent providing food stamps, medical care, and the like for the poorly-off. All that the utilitarian can defend, and it is easy to see that application of the utilitarian criterion for optimal institutions moves in the direction of economic equality for all. It is true, of course, that the utilitarian does not take equality as an end in itself; he moves in the direction of equality only because maximizing the general welfare can be attained only by more equality. The utilitarian also does not favor taking steps which would diminish the general welfare just for the sake of equality —for instance, giving a great deal of extra income to a disabled person in order to make up to him for his natural disability. Neither, incidentally, as far as I can see, does Rawls' theory. When we see how far a utilitarian theory does take us toward economic equality, we can well wonder how much farther the critic of utilitarianism would like to go. How large a percentage of the gross national product would he want diverted for the achievement of more equality than the utilitarian would ask for, and exactly how would he want it distributed? I suggest that when we reflect on how much economic equality we want in society, we shall not think that the implications of utilitarianism fall short. Many attacks on utilitarianism suppose that we are in a position to distribute happiness, not money—and it is said that a utilitarian must be oblivious of any inequalities in happiness, however great, so long as the maximum amount of happiness has been produced. This charge, however, while true, ignores the fact that the utilitarian theory does provide against severe deprivation of happiness, as in the case of a disabled person, on the ground that such provision is the best investment of national resources. The charge also ignores the fact that we are in no position to determine exactly what the relative levels of happiness of people are, and whether reasonably accurate equality-producing distributions could be entrusted, say to rationing boards, with distributive powers. So, at most this charge of the critics remains on a highly ideal level of speculation about what ought to be done if only someone knew the facts about relative welfare levels and what redistributions would remove the inequalities of welfare. I do not myself think that such charges need be taken very seriously. So, as far as I can see, the response of the utilitarian to the charge of an unsatisfactory theory of distributive justice comes off very well.

FOOTNOTES

1. *Sovran Maxims*, cited by Diogenes Laertius, nos. 31 and 37.

2. Mill seems not to have reflected on these puzzles as much as he should have. He says an act is wrong only if it is desirable that it be penalized somehow, either by law, or public opinion, or the individual's own conscience. He threw all three of these in together, as if he did not have to worry about conflicts. However, it might be expedient for the law to impose a fine for overparking, or for failing to make a certain type of report about the assets of one's company; but it is far from clear that we would want to make these requirements of conscience, except insofar as conscience may tell us that there is a presumption that the law is to be obeyed. At any rate, overparking and failing to make required reports do not appear to be immoral in themselves. What Mill should have said, I think, is that something is morally wrong if it is a token of an act-type for which it is desirable that the agent be penalized by his own conscience, or is one which his own conscience should motivate him to avoid, or disapprove of in others, on utilitarian grounds.

3. J.L. Mackie, *Ethics: Inventing Right and Wrong*, 1977, p. 150.

4. Actually, one could argue with some force that Mill, who is supposed to be a hedonist, was straddling the two theories, for

he takes the odd view that virtue and wealth are *parts* of happiness. He has often been accused of confusion here, and doubtless he was confused. What he had good reason for saying was only that people *want* such things as money and virtue, and may be made unhappy by not obtaining them. Could he have confused being desired and being pleasant? On a later page he seems to confirm such a confusion by saying that "desiring a thing and finding it pleasant . . . are two different modes of naming the same psychological fact" (*Utilitarianism*, ch. 4).

5. See James Griffin, "Is unhappiness more important than happiness?" *Philosophical Quarterly* 29 (1979), 47–55.

ON MORAL RIGHTS

A. I. Melden

1

On the whole, the notion that persons have moral rights has not fared well in philosophical circles. Consider, for example, the doctrine of natural, unalienable, or imprescriptable rights. Effective as this doctrine had proved to be in rallying men to the cause of liberty, it was nonetheless reviled, among others, by Jeremy Bentham, who characterized it as "nonsense upon stilts," an open invitation to anarchy to be consigned to the philosophic dustbin. Yet the view that human rights exist independently of any institutional arrangements, Bentham's contrary view notwithstanding, has played too important a practical role to be ignored altogether; and in recent years that view has regained some measure of the philosophical respectability it enjoyed in the seventeenth and eighteenth centuries.

But even when philosophers have conceded that there are moral rights—whether these be those labeled "natural" or "human" or those special rights that vary with the particular circumstances of human life—the concessions made to them are very often little more than lip service paid to our everyday sense of their existence, without any appreciation of the conceptual ramifications of these rights or the role they play, or should play, in our moral thinking. Indeed, quite often the very existence of such rights has been glossed over by moral philosophers or completely ignored, even where these rights are of the very first importance to the issues under discussion.

No better example of this last point can be cited than the philosophical discussions of the obligation of promises. Here is a paradigm of a right-conferring transaction, one that played a central role in the attempts of such classical contract theorists as Hobbes and Locke to justify the exercise of political power. Yet when Hobbes addresses himself to the question of how it is that a promise obliges—a matter on which Locke is silent—he seems to be unaware that a promise confers a right when he declares that the breaking of a promise (or covenant) is analogous to

> . . . that which in the disputation of the Scholars is called absurdity. For it is there called an Absurdity to contradict

107

what one has maintained in the Beginning; so in the world, it is called Injustice and Injury, voluntarily to undo that, which from the beginning he has voluntarily done.[1]

I shall not review Hume's discussion in the *Treatise* of the obligation of promises. He tells us there that the common sense belief in the obligation of promises can be explained but cannot be justified, resting as it does upon self-deception, as much so as do the beliefs in personal identity and the independent existence of material objects.[2] My concern is rather with Prichard, who recognized the importance of the problem posed by Hume and struggled to resolve it.[3] Yet in his essay "Does Moral Philosophy Rest on a Mistake?", published much earlier in 1912, Prichard appears at one point to recognize a factor involved in certain of our moral obligations, only to fail to explore the matter further and apply it, as indeed one might have expected him to do, to the case of promises. For, the obligation to tell the truth, he tells us,

> . . . involves a relation consisting in the fact that others are trusting us to speak the truth, a relation the apprehension of which gives rise to the sense that communication of the truth is something owing by us to them.[4]

But the communication of the truth as something we owe to those to whom we speak, can only be, surely, the same thing which, viewed from the latter's point of view, is the entitlement, i.e., the right, they have to truthfulness from us. And if we do owe others truthfulness—correlatively, if those to whom we speak have a right to truthfulness and, as Prichard puts it, repose their trust in us—then surely a similar relation exists between those who give and receive promises. Promisers owe promisees what they have promised them they will do, as much so as language users owe "the communication of the truth" to those to whom they speak; and promisees, generally at least, trust promisers to redeem their pledges just as those to whom we speak trust us to be truthful. But in Prichard's discussion of the obligation of promises there is no sense of the fact that a promise confers a right—in short, that it is *this* moral relation that is established between promiser and promisee, the complex conceptual features of which need to be detailed if the old problem of the obligation of promises is to be resolved. Instead, and with his characteristic myopia about human action generally, Prichard thinks that what we 'really' do when we promise is to make certain noises 'connected symbolically' with the action which, as we ordinarily say, we promise to perform; and the problem then becomes the insoluble problem of explaining how the making of such noises gives rise to any obligation—unless we assume, and this is admittedly unhelpful, that there is some general agreement, which somehow does not require the use of language, not to make such noises without going on to execute the relevant performances.

A similar suggestion surfaces but is never explored either by Prichard or by Ross during the course of the latter's efforts to explain the technical term "*prima facie* duty" introduced by him into the philosophical literature. During the course of his effort to explain what he means by this expression, Ross rejects a suggestion he reports that Prichard had made; namely, that instead of speaking of prima facie duties in connection with, say, promises, one should speak of claims.[5] For of course one person may have a claim on another in a situation in which there may be another competing claim that must prevail morally. But the notion of a claim that is relevant here is the notion, not of a claim that is *made*, but a claim that any individual *has* against another. And here it is difficult to see what such a claim could be if it is not indeed a right. Once more, the notion of a moral relation involving a right, with its correlative obligation, has surfaced only to be dismissed and remain unexplored. For this philosophical failure Ross has only himself to blame. He tells us that in the case in which one person has a claim on or against another, which the latter may honor by some performance, "ordinary language provides us with . . . no correlative to claim" that is appropriate to the point of view of the agent, this being the point of view the expression "prima facie duty" was designed to secure.[6] And surely this is a mistake. Here it is important to take note of the prepositional phrases that in ordinary speech often follow the words "obligation" and "duty"; for we not only speak of what it is that one ought, or has a duty, *to do*, but also of the obligation or duty one may have *to a person*, an obligation or duty that one can meet or discharge by according him the right he has against one. Why then should Ross, like Prichard before him, neglect this commonplace fact of usage to mark the moral relations between persons, relations which provide an explanation for that which they have been most insistent upon maintaining—namely, that the making of promises, like the making of declarations in statements we address to others *as such* and necessarily so—provides a reason for the relevant moral requirement: in the one case for redeeming the pledges we have made, in the other for speaking what is honestly in our minds. It is not, in my opinion, the neglect of linguistic usage or even the craving for philosophical generality that lead Ross and Prichard to employ the blanket terms "obligation" or "duty" to cover not only the moral relations between persons but the requirements of action as well. It is, rather, the constricted view of morality itself as a matter having to do mainly if not exclusively with what it is that one ought to do, that is the source of the failure to notice the characteristic idioms we employ; and it is *this* narrow view of morality that is responsible for their oblivion to the important and complex moral relations that bind promiser and promisee, speaker and addressee, and so on in other instances in which there are rights and their correlative obligations.

In the case of Kant—ironically a stalwart defender of the rights of man—this same constricted view of the nature of morality is evidenced in his attempt in the *Foundations* to subsume considerations which plainly *do* involve a consideration of rights and their correlative obligations, along with considerations that do not, under what he takes to be the morally fundamental concept of duty. The duty so-called of beneficence does not involve any right to the help we ought to give others; but this is labeled "an imperfect duty" on the ground that it turns on inclination: the desire for help by those who now need it and the fact that anyone, including those who provide such help, will themselves need and want the assistance of others. The duty of promise-keeping, of preserving one's life or of telling the truth, would appear to involve rights; but this distinctive feature of such 'duties' is wholly obscured by Kant's labeling them "perfect duties" on the ground that inclinations are wholly irrelevant.[7] And the subsumption of both sorts of moral requirements under the concept of duty, i.e., of what one is duty-bound to do by virtue of the moral law, once more is to take as central the notion of what we ought, or are duty bound, to do, and to ignore those complex moral relations between particular individuals constituted by their rights and their correlative obligations.

2

It is, of course, a familiar fact that the right established by a promise is not like a bank draft that is payable on demand, but

a right that in special circumstances, for good and sufficient
reason, must be infringed. Many have therefore applied the
qualifying expression "prima facie" to rights just as Ross applied
it to duty—for just as one may say quite correctly "One ought to
tell the truth, but in this situation I am duty-bound to conceal
it," so one may say "I know that you have a right to such-and-
such, but it would be morally wrong for me here and now to accord it to you." I shall not here discuss at length this use of the
qualifying expression "prima facie" except to remark that no
reputable philosopher of the past, certainly not Locke, has ever
maintained that anyone may demand, assert, or exercise any
right that he may have, just as it may suit his fancy and no matter what the circumstances may be. Locke, concerned as he was
that sovereigns might abuse their authority—a matter that
troubled him far more than the possibility that individuals in
civil society might create social havoc if allowed the liberty to
pursue their fortunes free from any interference—takes note of
the fact that, even if we grant that sovereigns have powers, i.e.,
the authority provided by their rights—authority comparable to
those absolute powers of military commanders in the field who,
as we say, have the power of life or death over their subordi-
nates—their power "is not arbitrary by being absolute, but is
still limited by that reason, and confined to those ends which
required it in some cases to be absolute."[8] For an absolute right
is a right that human beings have, *qua* human beings and not,
as in the case of such special rights as those enjoyed by promisees, on the condition that there are certain social circumstances, e.g., the prior occurrence of a promise-transaction. And
there is nothing in Locke's *Second Treatise* to suggest the view
that there are any absolute rights in that mindless sense according to which, given that one has a right, one may do as one
pleases, others being duty-bound never to interfere with the exercise of that right no matter what the circumstances. Indeed,
Locke is quite specific not only in the passage I have cited, but
in his discussions of the right to property, where he maintains
that there are rational constraints that must be observed by
anyone acquiring property.[9]

The point I want to make, however, is that the use of "prima
facie" not only serves no useful function—for any right, human
or special, may be justifiably infringed or reasonably limited in
the way it is exercised—but also that the widespread use of this
expression has been downright pernicious. For the fact that,
say, a promisee has a right, is one thing, and the fact that the

right may or may not succeed in justifying the obligation-
meeting act is quite another. And to speak for that reason of the
right itself as prima facie—even to suggest, as some have, that it
is a right in a different sense, or even that it is an 'absolute' right
when it does succeed in this justificatory role—is not only to pile
one confusion upon another, but, by focusing our attention
narrowly upon the issue of whether or not a right succeeds in
fully justifying a given item of conduct, diverts our attention
from what needs to be firmly kept in view, namely, the complex
conceptual features of rights. For unless we attend to these features we are likely to miss some of the important ways in which
rights operate in our thought and action, and even why and
how it is that rights, which are indeed grounds for action, may
yet fail to be sufficient.[10]

For to understand that a person has a right, say by virtue of a
promise, involves much more than the sense that the person
who has given his word is under an obligation to that person, or
even that this obligation may be overridden. It involves the
understanding of the ways in which the lives of the two—
promiser and promisee—are connected because of the promise
transaction that has taken place. This is not to say that persons
cannot promise in bad faith or that those who receive and acknowledge such persons may not be or may not become indifferent to or forgetful of the promises they have received—allow-
ing those who have solemnly promised to remain, as it were, on
the hook, while they themselves proceed to live their own
lives—indifferent to or oblivious of the heavy burdens of those
who remain bound to them. The point, rather, is that if we are
to gain a perspicuous view of the panoply of concepts in which
the concept of a right has its place, we must begin with those
paradigm cases in which morally responsible and morally sensitive agents are involved, agents who deal with each other in
good faith and in ways that reflect their awareness of whatever
moral burdens there are which they must bear not only with
respect to each other but to anyone else affected by their
conduct. And in the case of those rights and obligations created
by promises, we need to consider central or paradigm cases—not
those promises to do what is trivial, impossible, immoral, or
those so-called promises made to oneself—but those in which
what is promised is manageable by the promiser and necessary if
the promisee is to pursue his interests successfully, enjoying the
goods these define as he carries out his plans.

What is formally established by means of a promise transaction is the understanding of both parties that the promiser will support the agency of the promisee by contributing a performance (or abstention) which the latter needs but cannot himself supply (or assume without question will be forthcoming), for the successful pursuit of his interests. Therefore, the promisee who accepts the promise and who trusts the promiser to make good his pledge, is assured that the performance (or abstention) referred to in the promise locution will be forthcoming, as much as he is assured of his own resources as agent in that line of conduct for the success of which the promised performance (or abstention) is required. The promiser is then as much aware as the promisee of the latter's dependence, for the successful pursuit of his interests, upon the promiser making good his word; and he understands as does the promissee that the failure to keep the promise will bring to collapse that line of conduct in which the other person proposes to engage—as much so as if, in the absence of any promise that one person may give to another, he were to interfere with the latter's efforts to carry out his plans and projects. To let a person down by failing to keep one's promise is to subvert his agency; it is tantamount to interfering with a person's endeavors. And if the former is a violation of a right it can only be because of the right that persons have to pursue their interests and, if successful, achieve the benefits therefrom. Unless this were so, the failure to redeem one's pledges would only be defeating the expectations of others, thereby causing them harm or the wasted effort expended by them in pursuing their interests. The failures would then be cause for regret, perhaps even for a sense of shame for not having spared them the labor and pains suffered by those who had banked on one's doing the sorts of things one had said one would do. But it would not be moral damage that one inflicted on others by violating their rights, nor would it invite any sense of guilt, not mere shame, for having subverted the agency of others by failing to redeem the pledges one had made. Nor would it be in order for those who had suffered disappointment or harm either to hold the offender to account for his failure or to forgive him at the sight of any distress he might feel. Sympathizing with him at the sight of his distress, they could only hope that he would be more attentive to the desires, wishes, and expectations of others, remaking his self in this way, but not purging himself of any guilt by making restitution or reparation or by suffering any feelings of remorse—for no moral rights were violated, however shamefully he had neglected the interests of others and caused them disappointment and hurt. Yet it is precisely these features of the moral failure incurred by those who break their solemn word to others that need to be understood; and this is possible only if we recognize that promises confer moral rights which depend upon the fundamental right of human beings to pursue their interests. For to promise is to underwrite, by the support one pledges, the agency of another; and one will in good conscience provide that support if and only if one will respect the right of persons as agents to pursue their interests, in the given instance, with the understanding that the support specified will be forthcoming.

A promise is a formal device employed in establishing this mutual understanding, but there are other ways in which this may be done. Language is employed for ever so many reasons, in some cases merely to satisfy idle curiosity; in many other cases, it is used during the course of practical activities to serve the purposes of those who engage in these activities. Those who ask for information trust those to whom they speak to tell the truth and often in circumstances in which it is clear to everyone concerned that the information is requested in order to achieve some good or avoid some evil. The man running along the road with a bleeding child in his arms, and stopping long enough to ask someone he encounters the way to the hospital, is not collecting idle information; and, in responding in good faith as that stranger does, there is an understanding, shared by both parties to this linguistic transaction, that the information will support the inquirer's interest in securing assistance for the injured child. There are other cases, too, of this mutual understanding of the support to be given and received which depend upon the distinctive features of the personal relations of individuals. It is understood by those related by the close ties of friendship or by those related as husband and wife, as parent and offspring, or as siblings, that they are to give each other the special consideration and treatment that is their due. Here there may or may not have occurred any single voluntary act, as in the example of the linguistic transaction mentioned above or in the case of promise transactions, upon which the special right and its correlative obligation depends—although in the case of the relation between husband and wife there is, usually, the prior promise "to love, honor and cherish." What is important, despite the claim frequently made that special rights always de-rive from voluntary acts, is the mutual understanding that de-rives from the ways in which the lives of those involved are joined, however this may have come about—an understanding that exists independently of any promises that may have been made. It would be absurd for someone, having lived for an ex-tended period of time as common-law husband, attending to his common-law wife just as ordinary responsible husbands do, to tell her that he was under no obligation to her on the ground that there had been no marriage ceremony and no marriage vow. Here, clearly, actions and thoughts—those involved in the ways in which they live their life together, a life they share—speak far more loudly than any words that may have been ut-tered in a marriage ceremony. In any case, in those instances in which the rights and their correlative obligations occur because of the intimate ways in which the persons involved have joined their lives, the agency which each characteristically supplies in support of the agency of the other, is not well defined nor is it explicitly specified as it generally is in the case of those relations established by means of promises. The manner in which spouses or friends join their lives and support each others' endeavors is plain enough to the persons involved even though some of the occasions for, and the nature of, the support appropriate to those occasions may be altogether unforeseen or unforeseeable. At best it would be a weak effort at humor for a husband to re-mark to his wife, as they stood on the deck of their sinking ship, that he owed her no special assistance, on the ground that their present unhappy situation involved could not have been fore-seen by either, nor could the support she now needed in order to survive.

3

The view presented above is that one paradigm case of per-sons related by rights and their correlative obligations is found in the instance of persons intimately related by love and affec-tion—an instance in which, as in the case of husband and wife, the mutual understanding existing between them is extensive and open-ended. But this is not to say that paradigm cases of *promises* are found only in these sorts of cases, although they *can* occur even here. Nor should we conclude from the fact that a mutual understanding exists between husband and wife independently of any promise that may have been made, that this understanding may not be itself suspect, given the unsatisfactory nature of their roles with respect to each other, as in the case of a domineering husband and a subservient, submissive wife. For the conduct that conforms to certain instances of mutual understanding may serve only to preserve a morally-askew arrangement in which the interests worthy of a human being have been washed out of a submissive wife and the interest of the husband in nursing his ego is gratified by his domination. In extreme cases in which the wife is a willing slave to every whim of her husband, the mutual understanding existing between them defeats any acceptable moral purpose, and the talk about moral rights and obligations in such cases is as inapplicable as in the case of a promise made and accepted to commit an immoral act. In less extreme cases there are rights and obligations, overruled as they should be by the efforts that a wife may and should make to improve her own lot and reject as improper her husband's understanding of how husbands and wives are to live together. But the paradigm cases in which rights and obligations rest upon the mutual understanding of the support that husband and wife are to give each other are those in which each respects the other, and in which the interests of each have been developed and are being pursued in ways that are worthy of human beings. Yet even this is likely to raise some philosophic eyebrows. In part, the reason for this is the tendency of writers to think of moral rights on the analogy with legal rights. This tendency has been aided and abetted, curiously enough, by Hume who in the *Enquiry* appears to treat justice (to which at least many of us, unlike Hume, would regard moral rights to be of central importance) as if it were a matter involving rules pertaining to contracts, the acquisition and transfer of property, inheritances, and so on—and who is led to the view that promises, for example, by which one person binds himself to another have no application in those cases in which individuals are bound by the close and intimate ties of affection as are intimate friends or the members of a closely knit family, who conduct their affairs with each other without resorting to such legal instruments as deeds, contracts, and the like.[11]

I shall not here inquire into what can be meant by that "unlimited generosity" which would rule out, according to Hume, the application of the so-called rules of justice—for surely if there are any interests that human beings have, distinct from that interest in furthering the interests of others (and there must be such interests or there could be no interests of anyone to be furthered by anyone else)—then there will be, inevitably, occasions on which the interests of different individuals will compete for satisfaction, even in the case of those individuals who are bound by the strongest ties of affection. Besides, those who love one another are not moved in every moment of their relationship by a continuous outpouring of passionate concern with each other's well-being; inevitably there are periods in which the relations of the two are marked by unconcern if not irritation, and in which each pursues his or her own interests in oblivion or neglect of the other's desires. And if, for no other reason than to resolve satisfactorily the competition of interests that does on occasion occur even in the case of individuals who love one another, there will be a need for promise-transactions, albeit relatively infrequently in comparison with those that occur in the relations between other parties—witness the familiar instance of the husband, weary after a long, hard day at the office, who promises to take his wife to the movies the next night if only he can stay home that night and relax. And surely even where interests do not compete, unsolicited promises are made, e.g., by the husband who promises to give his wife the dress he knows she yearns to wear, just as soon as he receives his next paycheck, where there is nothing he wants in exchange and no balancing in which he engages of his interests against hers. Indeed, it should be evident, just as soon as we think about it, that unlike the case of contracts for which there are legal sanctions, in consequence of which contracts can be entered into by those who are indifferent or personally unknown to one another, the everyday promise transaction is not entered into by those who are strangers to one another, and without serious cautions and reservations. And Hume's well-known view that the promiser "subjects himself to the penalty of never being trusted again in case of failure,"[12] by suggesting moral ostracism as the analogue, for the case of promises, of the legal penalties that apply in the case of contracts, simply obscures the most obvious moral facts: promisees who have been let down can and sometimes do acknowledge that those who broke their promises did so justifiably; promisees can and do forgive those who wrongly let them down; promises in general are *not* given and accepted by those who are unfamiliar to or casual acquaintances of one another; and promises are entered into even by those who are bound to one another by the very closest ties of love and affection. Indeed, as I shall argue later, there could be no sense of obligation created by a promise, no respecting of the right of the person to whom one had given one's word, unless there existed a concern with, and a willingness to contribute to, his well-being.

I want, first, however, to mention other doctrines that stand in opposition to the view I have advanced: that rights and their correlative obligations are instanced conspicuously in the personal relations of individuals who are bound by the closest ties of affection and love, and most strikingly so because these obligations are as extensive and open-ended as they are. And Kant must surely come to mind in this connection, in a twofold manner. First, there is Kant's insistence that the fundamental principles of morality require that we set aside as irrelevant those intimate personal relations in which we stand to others and consider them and ourselves not as the particular individuals they and we are, each with distinctive interests and personality, but as equals because of a common and quite abstract status as rational beings endowed with will. The philosophical descendent of this Kantian doctrine, with modifications of course, is to be found in the view recently expounded by Rawls, according to which the moral requirements imposed upon any individual derive from his impersonal status as a place-holder in an institution that satisfies certain principles of justice, principles that anyone would choose on behalf of everyone else, given that the choice would be made under a veil of ignorance that shuts off from his view as morally irrelevant anything that distinguishes him from, and which might bring him into conflict with, anyone else. It is not surprising, because of their common heritage, that the Rawlsian doctrine echoes the view expressed by Bradley that one ought to set aside one's own particular will in favor of the universal will that is embodied in one's station and its duties. Secondly, there is the Kantian insistence on the moral irrelevance of one's own inclinations, and in the case of what he labels perfect duties, e.g., the duties to keep promises, to tell the truth, and so forth, the irrelevance of anyone's inclinations in any issue of what one is morally requited to do. A more recent form of this view is to be found in Prichard's insistence that we must distinguish sharply between morality and virtue "as coordinate but independent forms of goodness," meaning that we should regard as quite independent the goodness of any action from the sense that we ought to do it (as in the instances of truth-telling or promise-keeping) as well as the goodness involved in doing something with a view to helping another or contributing to his or her well-being. And while Prichard goes on to say that moral goodness—restricted by him in characteristic Kantian fashion to the goodness of actions performed out of a sense of obligation—and virtue are "related species of goodness," he does not spell out the relation. And his language certainly implies that one's sense that one ought to perform an act, say, of promise-keeping is quite independent of any feelings, inclination, or desire that one might have for the well-being of the individual to whom one is under the given obligation—and, we might add, so too with the appreciation of the right that is the correlative of this obligation.[13]

I shall not attempt to review the writings of those who, unlike Kant and Prichard, are at pains to find a place for rights in our scheme of moral concepts, often because of the parallels they have come to recognize, between moral and legal rights; although it is worth noting that, in their concern to emphasize some of the distinctive features of the moral concept of rights, some have been led to suggest, at least, the kind of sharp distinction made by Prichard when they have argued that the concept of a moral right belongs to a quite different sphere or branch of morality from that of good or virtue.[14] It is this view, namely, that the sense of obligation we feel when we recognize the right of anyone, is free-wheeling with respect to our concern with that person's well-being, to which I shall now turn before examining the first of the two Kantian themes that stand in opposition to the view I have advanced.

4

Consider a paradigm case of a promise given and accepted in good faith by morally mature and sensitive agents, by which it is mutually understood that what is promised is required in order that some important interest might be successfully pursued by the promisee. That interest, and the good it defines, may or may not be known to the promiser, for one might solicit a promise without divulging the nature of one's interest in the matter; but we shall assume that interest not to be a trivial matter.

(a) A conscientious agent, having given his solemn word, surely is mindful of his promise during some period of time, often of some length, not infrequently adjusting his own affairs and modifying his own plans and projects in order to be able to comply at the appropriate time with the terms of his promise. But why should he alter in this manner that segment of his own life, in order, as we commonly put it, to live up to his pledge? For it is not only that promiser and promisee mutually understand that what is promised is required by the latter in order successfully to pursue his interest and achieve his good, but that wherever necessary the promiser will be mindful of this fact and, if need be, alter the tenor and pattern of some segment of his own life in order to keep his promise and thereby support the agency of the promisee. But why, to repeat, should the promiser, fully aware that this will be required of him, give his word, and why, having promised, will he proceed to comply in this way? Is it that, as some have suggested, a promise is a bargain from which both parties benefit in the making and the keeping of it? But often promises are given without any consideration of self-interest and, having been accepted by those to whom they are given; surely the interest in making good one's word may be simply a matter of good conscience. Why then should one be conscientious, as often one is, in so altering a segment of one's life, in thought and in action, that without undue exaggeration one can say that one has, during that period of time, joined one's life to that of the promisee in ensuring that one will support his endeavors, whatever it may be, in carrying out the terms of one's promise? Is it that good conscience requires that one do this in order to preserve the socially useful form of social transaction; or, as Rawls put it, the just or fair 'institution' of promising? But on neither of these views, all other objections aside, is there a moral right that the promisee has in this case (he has the right to certain expectations; but this locution can be translated, without invoking the language of moral rights, into what it is that he would be justified in expecting); on neither of these views is there any room for any right to the particular performance that has been promised. For the promiser, however much he ought to promote social utility or just institutions is, in addition, bound *to the person to whom he has promised.* Why, then, should he, as the reasonable and conscientious agent he is, adjust his own affairs and stand ready to meet his obligation unless he is concerned with the interests and goods these define—in short, with the well-being of the person with whom he has joined some segment of his own life? The right (and its correlative obligation) does indeed justify the obligation-meeting action, whatever it might be; but the conscientious promiser could not adjust his own life to the interest, whatever this might be, of the promisee, out of his sense of the latter's right (and that sense of his obligation to him) unless the latter's interests and the goods these define were a matter of genuine concern to him.

(b) The same conclusion is forced upon us if we consider one's sense of guilt for having violated someone's right. And here we need to think of morally mature and responsible individuals, not psychopaths devoid of any sense of obligation who parrot without understanding the promise-locutions normal persons employ, or those morally parochial individuals whose sense of obligation is restricted to those who are members of their in-group and for whom accordingly deception and bad faith toward the stranger or outsider is a socially approved way of life. For in order to understand such deviant cases we need to understand the promise-transactions they simulate or those they fall short of; namely, those performed in good faith and with an understanding of what it is that they involve. And in the case of those who, as morally mature and responsible individuals, promise in good faith, there are those occasioned lapses in which, forgetful perhaps of what it is that they have promised to do, or succumbing to temptation at the critical moment, they let down those who have trusted them. Here, clearly, there is no mere regret the person at fault feels when he comes to reflect on his moral failure, nor mere sympathetic distress at the sight of the frustrations and unhappiness of those who, as we say, have only themselves to blame for their failure to advance their own interests. For the pangs of guilt, as phenomena of normal human life and not as manifestations of some deep-seated pathological condition of the self, are morally healthy; they are the painful experiences of one who views the distress of someone else as *his* doing, as the moral damage for which *he* is responsible. The person who recognizes his guilt in the matter, as a failure on his part to vindicate the trust the morally injured party had reposed in him, feels deeply and painfully that he is flawed and unworthy of the respect the injured party had previously accorded him, and unworthy, too, of the ties with him that he had enjoyed in the past. But this surely involves caring for the other person, a concern with the well-being of one whose good will and respect he had enjoyed and reciprocated in the

past, but of which he now feels unworthy. And it is for this reason that he feels the need to purge himself of his guilt, to make
reparation for the injury he has caused, and to demonstrate by
whatever means available that he is worthy of the forgiveness
that will restore the good will of the one he has let down.

In short, the sense of guilt of those who have transgressed
against others by violating the right conferred upon them by
their promises—like the manner in which those who consci-
entiously alter the character of their thought and action during
the parts of their lives in which they stand prepared to support
the endeavors of those to whom they have given their solemn
pledges—would be unreasonable without a concern on their
part to further the interests of those to whom they are bound
and thereby promote the goods those interests define. Far from
it being the case, as Prichard thought—that the goodness of
conscientious obligation-meeting conduct is independent of the
goodness of other-regarding action—a conscientious and morally sensitive agent could not act as he does without a concern
for the well-being of anyone to whom he is morally bound. No
doubt there are unthinking souls who have never outgrown the
crusty moral habits of their social group and for whom conscientious behavior so-called is often devoid of the leavening influence of any benevolent feelings toward those to whom they
are in fact morally bound. But there is no more reason to think
of such instances of imperfect development as models of moral
achievement than there is to regard those who urge that we
obey the law because it is sacred (or because it *is* the law) as
storehouses of legal wisdom. But for those who *are* sensitive to
the relevant features of the moral relations in which they stand
to others, a reflective consideration of the special ways in which
they are morally bound to others *does* imply a concern to advance their interests and thereby promote their well-being.

5

I turn now to the other Kantian theme: that in considering
our obligations to others—the rights they have against us—we
are to ignore as morally irrelevant the quite intimate personal
relations in which, quite often, we stand to them, and that we
are to deal with them impersonally—a view echoed by such
moral institutionalists as Bradley and Rawls. And, here, in considering the example of the rights and obligations created by

promise-transactions, I want to focus attention upon the moral burdens assumed by both promisee and promiser.

Having promised, I am mindful of my obligation, arrange my affairs as necessary and stand prepared to redeem the pledge I have given. But, as all of us know, circumstances may change unexpectedly, and so indeed do the persons to whom we are bound; and what may have been vital to the important interests of the promisee are no longer of any consequence to him, given the change in his circumstances, and even in the character of his own plans and projects as old interests fade and new ones take their place. Besides, what may have been quite manageable on my part as the promise-keeping action, unforeseeably comes to be unusually burdensome to me even as, because of the unexpected changes that occur in the circumstances and the interests of the person to whom I have promised, the promised action becomes less and less important to him. Indeed, although quite manageable by me in my present condition, and even if the keeping of the promise remains a matter of importance to the promisee, there are others—those to whom I am also bound and who along with the promisee depend upon my support for the successful pursuit of *their* interests. And there may be human beings I encounter, and to whom I have no special moral obligation, who need, desperately so if they are to survive and not merely to meet the special obligations in which they stand to others, the help that I can give them, far more so than does the person to whom I had given my pledge. So there are decisions that need to be made by me, hard ones on occasion, in deciding how, in the light of all of the circumstances of my case, to respond to the right of the promisee, and to anyone else seriously affected by my conduct. And there are decisions that the promisee himself may have to make in responding to what it is I have been led to do and to how it is that I respond to him in the event I do not accord him his right. What is particularly objectionable about the philosophical talk about prima facie rights and obligations, and the picture of an agent weighing one of these against others, is that it tends to obscure from our view the complication of possible circumstances that must enter our reflections and the reasons why they affect as they do our responses to the moral situation in which, on occasion and unexpectedly, we find ourselves.

Earlier I said that each of us, as human beings, has a right to pursue his or her interests and that a promisee has a right to the promised action, since whatever the line of conduct may be in which he pursues some interest of some importance, and by which if he is successful he achieves some good that is defined by that interest, it is understood by both parties that support for his endeavors is to be provided by the promised action. Promisers, accordingly, will respect the right of promisees as human beings to pursue their interests if and only if they respect the rights the latter have against them as the recipients of promises. And, as I have just argued, promisers will be mindful of and concerned with their moral relations to promisees only if they are concerned with those interests and those goods of promisees upon which their promises have a bearing. But if, unexpectedly, those interests have faded—if there are other and more important matters that concern them now in ways not foreseen by them earlier when the promises were made; or if, again unexpectedly, the important interests of still other persons to whom promisers are also bound, or, their own important interests in the plans and projects in which they have been involved will be adversely affected—then these interests and the goods they define will be brought into view, along with the interests and the goods to which their promises are relevant, as relevant practical considerations. This is not to say that the fact that anyone has an interest in something, and if successful in his efforts to achieve it, will establish his right to whatever help anyone can provide him. It is rather to say that, given that he does have such a right, the question whether he still has any interest relevant to the promised action is a consideration that needs to be taken into account by anyone considering whether or not to keep his promise. And it is to say, further, that in deciding whether or not to perform the promised action, we are not to consider as irrelevant any unexpected impact that action has on one's own interests or on those of parties other than promiser or promisee who have rights against us.[15]

This is one of the sorts of considerations one might weigh in deciding whether or not to meet one's obligation by keeping one's promise. And just as it may justify one in infringing the right of another, so it may justify the possessor of a right, given this understanding of the relevant circumstances, in waiving or even relinquishing the right that he has against someone else. Moral rights are not those side-constraints or moral blinders that confine us—those who possess them or those against whom others have them—to those courses of action by which these rights are automatically exercised or accorded.

A second consideration that enters into our moral thinking is that our good moral relations with others may not be jeopardized or destroyed by our decisions not to accord others the rights they have against us. Hence it is that explanations need to be given to those, morally bound as we are to them, whose rights we must infringe; and hence it is that those to whom such explanations are given would be morally reprehensible in ignoring these explanations and in standing on their rights. Further, moral thinking is not a kind of moral geometry in which differences in the conclusions reached establish that error and incompetence has occurred. For reasonable men may differ, yet morally respect each other despite the differences to which they are led, and demonstrate to each other their continued willingness to maintain, with mutual good will and trust, their good moral relations with each other. And even where error, evident to any reasonable person, has occurred, and even where temptation and self-deception have led to unjustified infringements of the rights of others, those whose rights have been denied are required to forgive those who have transgressed against them, given the appropriate indications of the remorse that has purged them of their guilt.

But a third consideration that must enter into our moral reflections—a consideration to which I alluded earlier—must not be forgotten. For the right of human beings to pursue their interests is no mere liberty, with respect to which the only obligation of others is to abstain from interference. For a right calls for a setting in which that right may be enjoyed; otherwise, like the right to be free which in extreme circumstances degenerates into the freedom to live in squalor, the right to pursue one's interest will be the right of those who are deprived of any opportunity to acquire interests in accordance with their native abilities and to develop the skills they need in our society, to huddle in misery and ignorance in lives that are not worthy of human beings.

In respect of all three of the above considerations it is manifest, however, that if morally we are to acquit ourselves well, we shall have to take account of the particular features of those individuals to whom we are related by our moral rights and obligations. Human beings do not come out of the same mold, with the same interests and the same goods that play the same role in the same plans and projects. For moral purposes, persons are not faceless place-holders in institutional arrangements, to deal with and to be dealt by others in terms defined by those institutional rights and duties that define their offices; they are, rather, individuals each with his or her distinctive personality. First, then, the measures of the importance of their interests, and the goods these define, cannot be taken independently of the particular pattern of their lives; and the closer our ties with them the more sensitive we shall be to which things matter for them and which, indeed, matter for them most. Second, how we shall deal with them in maintaining our good moral relations with them will reflect our sense of their temperaments, the degree of their patience or lack of it, with which they tolerate the misdemeanors and transgressions of others, our sense of their readiness or not (and to whatever degree it may exist) to adopt the points of view of others, to accept their explanations and, if need be, to forgive and forget. And, third, we must do whatever we need to do for others—recognizing the differences that exist between us, and mindful too of a variety of cautions that need to be observed in according them their rights as human beings—by providing for them the setting appropriate for their enjoyment, thus demonstrating our willingness to enter into personal relations with them—relations of the sort that we maintain with those relatively few persons to whom we are bound by the ties of love and friendship. In this way we widen, as far as it is possible for unsaintly persons like ourselves to do so, the circle of those who are morally bound to us, as we are to them, in these personal relations through which we connect our own lives with theirs.

FOOTNOTES

1. *Leviathan*, chapter 14.

2. Cf. *Treatise*, Bk. III, Pt. II, chap. V, "The Obligation of Promises."

3. Cf. his essay "The Obligation to Keep a Promise," written circa 1940 and published in *Moral Obligation*, Oxford: The Clarendon Press.

4. Ibid., pp. 8–9.

5. *The Right and the Good*, chap. II.

6. Ibid., p. 20.

7. See Kant's discussion of the four cases to which he applies the principle of the categorical imperative in the Second Selection of the *Foundations*.

8. *Second Treatise of Civil Government*, chap. XI, par. 139.

9. See for example his discussion of the restrictions in the amounts of property one might acquire in chap. V, par. 19. These, as I read Locke, are not ad hoc provisos, but intrinsic to our understanding of what is involved in the right to acquire property.

10. For a discussion of these issues see my *Rights and Persons*, especially chapters I and II.

11. See *An Enquiry Concerning the Principles of Morals*, Sec. III, "Of Justice."

12. *A Treatise of Human Nature*, Bk. III, P. II, Sec. 5, p. 522 of the Selby-Bigge edition.

13. Cf. his essay "Does Moral Philosophy Rest on a Mistake" in *Moral Obligation*, Oxford: The Clarendon Press, 1949.

14. See, for example, H.L.A. Hart in "Are There Natural Rights," *Philosophical Review*, April 1955, esp. pp. 177ff. I say "suggests," for he certainly does not explicitly address himself to the Prichardian thesis.

15. To simplify, I ignore here the fact that even moral rights may give way in the face of sufferings of animals to whom the ascription of moral rights is at best problematic.

Bibliography

Charles L. Stevenson

I. PUBLICATIONS

Books

1. *Ethics and Language.* New Haven: Yale University Press, 1944.
2. *Facts and Values.* New Haven: Yale University Press, 1963.

Articles

1. "The Emotive Meaning of Ethical Terms." *Mind* 46 (1937): 14–31.
2. "Ethical Judgments and Avoidability." *Mind* 47 (1938): 45–57.
3. "Persuasive Definitions." *Mind* 47 (1938): 331–350.
4. "Moore's Arguments against Certain Forms of Ethical Natural-ism." In *The Philosophy of G. E. Moore*, edited by P. A. Schilpp. Evanston: Northwestern University Press, 1942.
5. "Some Relations between Philosophy and the Study of Language." *Analysis* 9 (1947): 1–16.
6. "Meaning: Descriptive and Emotive." *Philosophical Review* 57 (1948): 127–144.
7. "The Nature of Ethical Disagreement." In *Readings in Philosophical Analysis*, edited by H. Feigl and W. Sellars. New York: Appleton-Century, 1949, pp. 587–593.
8. "Interpretation and Evaluation in Aesthetics." In *Essays in Philosophical Analysis*, edited by Max Black. Ithaca: Cornell University Press, 1949.
9. "The Emotive Conception of Ethics and its Cognitive Implica-tions." *Philosophical Review* 59 (1950): 291–304.
10. "Brandt's Questions about Emotive Ethics." *Philosophical Review* 59 (1950): 528–534.
11. "The Scientist's Role and the Aims of Education." *Harvard Educa-tional Review*, Fall 1954: 231–238.
12. Comments on a paper by Brandt. In *The Language of Value*, edited by Ray Lepley, pp. 317–323. New York: Columbia University Press, 1957.

13. "On 'What is a Poem?'" *Philosophical Review*, July 1957: 329–362.

14. "On the 'Analysis' of a Work of Art." *Philosophical Review*, January 1958: 33–51.

15. "Symbolism in the Non-Representational Arts," and "Symbolism in the Representational Arts." Chapters in *Language, Thought and Culture*, edited by Paul Henle. Ann Arbor: The University of Michigan Press, 1958.

16. "On the Reasons that can be Given for the Interpretation of a Poem." In *Philosophy Looks at the Arts*, edited by Joseph Margolis, pp. 121–139. New York: Scribners, 1962.

17. "Reflections on John Dewey's Ethics." *Proceedings of Aristotelian Society* 1961–62: 25–44.

18. "Relativism and Nonrelativism in the Theory of Value." *Proceedings of the American Philosophical Association* 1961–62.

19. "Ethical Fallibility." In *Ethics and Society*, edited by Richard T. DeGeorge, pp. 197–217. Garden City, NY: Anchor Books, 1966.

20. "The Rhythm of English Verse." *Journal of Aesthetics and Art Criticism*, Spring 1970: 327–344.

21. "Richards on the Theory of Value." In *I. A. Richards: Essays in his Honor*, edited by Brower, Vendler, and Hollander, pp. 119–134. Fair Lawn, NJ: Oxford University Press, 1973.

22. "A Reply to Professor Wheeler's 'Disagreement in Belief About Interests'." *Southwest Journal of Philosophy* 8 (Winter 1977): 530.

II. CRITICAL COMMENT

Aiken, Henry. "Emotive 'Meanings' and Ethical Terms." *Journal of Philosophy* (1944): 456–70.

Baier, Kurt. "Fact, Value and Norm in Stevenson's Ethics." *Nous* 1 (May 1967): 139–160.

Blankemeyer, Kenneth J. "Can Reliance on Quasi-Dependent Meaning Save Stevenson's Ethics?" *Journal of Thought* 12 (January 1977): 26–30.

Dewey, John. "Ethical Subject-Matter and Language." *The Journal of Philosophy* XLII (December 20, 1945): 701–712.

Foster, Lawrence. "Inductive and Ethical Validity." *American Philosophical Quarterly* 8 (January 1971): 35–44.

Gouinlock, James. "Dewey's Theory of Moral Deliberation." *Ethics* 88 (April 1978): 218–228.

Hudson, W. D. *A Century of Moral Philosophy*. New York: St. Martin's Press, 1980, pp. 105–124.

Kerner, George C. *The Revolution in Ethical Theory*, Chapter II. New York: Oxford University Press, 1966, pp. 40–96.

Martin, R. M. "On Stevenson's 'If-iculties'." *Philosophy of Science* 39 (December 1972): 515–521.

McClintock, Thomas. "Moore and Stevenson On A Certain Form of Ethical Naturalism." *Personalist* 52 (Summer 1971): 432–448.

Roberts, George W. "Some Refutations of Private Subjectivism In Ethics." *Journal of Value Inquiry* 5 (Winter 1971): 292–309.

Thomas, Vincent. "Ethical Disagreement and Emotive Theory of Values." *Mind* LX (April 1951): 205–222.

Walter, Edward F. "Empiricism and Ethical Reasoning." *American Philosophical Quarterly* 7 (1970): 364–378.

Wellman, Carl. "Emotivism and Ethical Objectivity." *American Philosophical Quarterly* V (April 1968): 90–99.

Wheeler, Arthur M. "Disagreement in Belief About Interests." *Southwest Journal of Philosophy* 8 (Winter 77): 49–51.

_____. "A Reply to Professor Stevenson's a Reply to Professor Wheeler's *Disagreement in Belief About Interests*." *Southwest Journal of Philosophy* 8 (Winter 77): 55–57.

III. RELATED BOOKS AND ARTICLES

Ayer, Alfred J. *Language, Truth and Logic*, Chapter VI. New York: Dover Publications, 1952.

Blanshard, Brand. "The New Subjectivism In Ethics." *Philosophy and Phenomenological Research* 9 (1949): 504–511. [Criticizes subjectivism on both analytic and moral grounds.]

_____. The Impasse in Ethics and a Way Out. *University of California Publications in Philosophy* 28 (1954): 92–112.

Falk, W. D. "Goading and Guiding." *Mind* LXII (April 1953): 141–171. [Distinguishes rational from nonrational means of persuasion. Thinks this distinction is overlooked by the emotivists.]

Feigel, Hebert. "De Principiis Non Disputandum . . . ?" In *Philosophical Analysis*, edited by Max Black, pp. 113–147. Ithaca: Cornell University Press, 1950. [Comments on the extent to which justification in ethics is and is not possible.]

Findlay, J. N. "The Justification of Attitudes." *Mind* LXIII (April 1954): 145–161. [Contends that attitudes can be justified—that there can be a logic of the heart.]

Jensen, H. "Hume on Moral Agreement." *Mind* 86 (October 1977): 497–513. [Criticizes Stevenson's interpretation of Hume on the issue of moral agreement. Defends a view characterized as ethical agnosticism against what he characterizes as Frankena's ethical fideism.]

Mackie, John. "A Refutation of Morals." XXIV *Australasian Journal of Psychology and Philosophy* (Sept. 1946): 77–90. [Criticizes objective theory of ethics.]

Prior, A. N. "Escapism: The Logical Basis of Ethics." *Essays in Moral Philosophy*, edited by A. I. Melden, pp. 135–146. Seattle: University of Washington, 1958.

Stroll, Avrum. "The Emotive Theory of Ethics." *University of California Publications in Philosophy* 28 (1954): 1–92.

"The Emotive Theory of Ethics." *Aristotelian Society Suppl.* vol. XXII (1948): 79–140. [Articles by Richard Robinson 79–186, H. J. Paton 107–126, R. C. Cron, 127–140. On Saturday, July 10 at 8 P.M., the Aristotelian Society in conjunction with The Mind Association conducted a symposium on "The Emotive Theory of Ethics." Professor Robinson criticizes Sir David Ross's analysis of "good" and defends the emotivist program. Professor Paton criticizes Robinson's account and explicitly raises the issue of whether or not the emotivists undermine ethics. Professor Cron is also critical but on analytic grounds. Cron has the most explicit references to Stevenson's *Ethics and Language*.]

Whittemore, Robert C. "Positivistic Paths To Value." *Tulane Studies in Philosophy* 21 (1972): 159–190.

William K. Frankena

I. PUBLICATIONS

Books

1. *Ethics*. Englewood Cliffs, New Jersey: Prentice-Hall, Inc., 1963. Second Edition, 1973.

2. (Editor) *Philosophy of Education*. New York: Macmillan, 1965.

3. *Three Historical Philosophies of Education*. Chicago: Scott, Foresman, 1965.

4. (Editor and Introduction with co-editor Arnold S. Kaufman). Jonathan Edwards, *Freedom of the Will*. Library of Liberal Arts, Indianapolis and New York: Bobbs-Merrill, 1969.

5. (Co-editor, with John T. Granrose). *Introductory Readings in Ethics.* Englewood Cliffs, New Jersey: Prentice-Hall, Inc., 1974.

6. (Author, with Uwsei Temkin). *Respect for Life In Medicine, Philosophy and the Law.* Baltimore: Johns Hopkins University Press, 1977.

7. *Thinking About Morality.* Ann Arbor: University of Michigan Press, 1980.

Articles

1. "The Naturalistic Fallacy." *Mind* 48 (1939): 464–477. Reprinted in several anthologies.

2. "Obligation and Value in the Ethics of G. E. Moore." In *The Philosophy of G. E. Moore*, edited by P. A. Schilpp, pp. 91–110. LaSalle, Illinois: Open Court Publishing Co., 1942.

3. "Our Belief in Reason." *Papers of the Michigan Academy of Science, Arts and Letters* 19 (1943): 571–586.

4. "Ewing's Case Against Naturalistic Theories of Value." *Philosophical Review* 57 (1948): 481–492.

5. "Arguments for Non-Naturalism About Intrinsic Value." *Philosophical Studies* 1 (1950): 56–60.

6. "Obligation and Ability." In *Philosophical Analysis*, edited by Max Black, pp. 157–175. Ithaca, New York: Cornell University Press, 1950.

7. "Moral Philosophy at Mid-Century." *Philosophical Review* 60 (1951): 44–55.

8. "The Concept of Universal Human Rights." In *Science, Language and Human Rights.* Volume I, Symposia, Eastern Division, American Philosophical Association, 1952, pp. 189–207.

9. "Sellars' Theory of Valuation." *Philosophy and Phenomenological Research* 15 (1954): 65–81.

10. "Hutcheson's Moral Sense Theory." *Journal of the History of Ideas* 16 (1955): 356–375.

11. "Natural and Inalienable Rights." *Philosophical Review* 64 (1955): 212–232.

12. "Towards a Philosophy of the Philosophy of Education." *Harvard Educational Review* 26 (1956): 94–98.

13. "Ethical Naturalism Renovated." *Review of Metaphysics* 10 (1957): 457–473.

14. "Moral Philosophy in America." In *Encyclopedia of Morals*, edited by Vergilius Ferm, pp. 348–360. New York: Philosophical Library, Inc., 1957.

15. "Henry Sidgwick." In *Encyclopedia of Morals*, edited by Vergilius Ferm, pp. 534–544. New York: Philosophical Library, Inc., 1957.

16. "Sir (William) David Ross." In *Encyclopedia of Morals*, edited by Vergilius Ferm, pp. 504–511. New York: Philosophical Library, Inc., 1957.

17. "Ethics, 1949–1955." In *Philosophy in the Mid-Century: A Survey*, Volume III, edited by R. Klibansky, pp. 42–77. Florence: Nuova Italia, 1958.

18. "MacIntyre on Defining Morality." *Philosophy* 33 (1958): 158–162.

19. "Obligation and Motivation in Recent Moral Philosophy." In *Essays in Moral Philosophy*, edited by A. I. Melden, pp. 40–81. Seattle: University of Washington Press, 1958.

20. "A Point of View for the Future." In *Religion and the State University*, edited by E. A. Walter, pp. 295–309. Ann Arbor: University of Michigan Press, 1958.

21. "Some Aspects of Language and "'Cognitive' and 'Non-Cognitive'." In *Language, Thought and Culture*, edited by Paul Henle, pp. 121–172. Ann Arbor: University of Michigan Press, 1958.

22. "Toward a Philosophy of Moral Education." *Harvard Educational Review* 28 (1958): 300–313.

23. "Broad's Analysis of Ethical Terms." In *The Philosophy of C. D. Broad*, edited by P. A. Schilpp, pp. 537–562. New York: Tudor Publishing Co., 1959.

24. "The Teaching of Religion: Some Guiding Principles." *Religious Education* 54 (1959): 108–109.

25. "Ethics in an Age of Science." *The Association of Princeton Alumni, Report of the Eighth Conference*, 1960: 91–104.

26. Foreword in Jonathan Edwards, *On the Nature of True Virtue*. Ann Arbor: University of Michigan Press, 1960. Ann Arbor Paperbacks.

27. "Is the Philosophy of Education Intellectually Responsible?" *Proceedings of the Philosophy of Education Society* 17 (1961): 36–45.

28. "Public Education and the Good Life." *Harvard Educational Review* 30 (1961): 413–426.

29. "The Concept of Social Justice." In *Social Justice*, edited by R. B. Brandt, pp. 1–29. Englewood Cliffs, New Jersey: Prentice-Hall, Inc., 1962.

30. "Lewis' Imperatives of Right." *Philosophical Studies* 14 (1963): 25–28.

31. "Recent Conceptions of Morality." In *Morality and the Language of*

Conduct, edited by H. N. Castaneda and G. Nakhnikian, pp. 1–24. Detroit: Wayne State University Press, 1963.

32. "Decisionism and Separatism in Social Philosophy." In *Nomos VII: Rational Decision*, edited by C. J. Friedrich, pp. 18–25. New York: Atherton Press, 1964.

33. "Ethical Theory." In *Philosophy*, edited by R. Schlatter, pp. 345–363. Humanities Scholarship in America: The Princeton Studies. Englewood Cliffs, New Jersey: Prentice-Hall, Inc., 1964.

34. "C. I. Lewis on the Ground and Nature of the Right." *Journal of Philosophy* 61 (1964): 489–496.

35. "Love and Principle in Christian Ethics." In *Faith and Philosophy*, edited by Alvin Plantinga, pp. 203–225. Grand Rapids, Michigan: William B. Eerdmans Publishing Co., 1964.

36. "On Defining and Defending Natural Law." In *Law and Philosophy*, edited by Sidney Hook, pp. 200–209. New York: New York University Press, 1964.

37. "La philosophie moral contemporaine aux Etats-Unis." *Les Etudes Philosophiques* 2 (1964): 233–243.

38. "Three Comments on Lewis's Views on the Right and the Good." *Journal of Philosophy* 61 (1964): 567–570.

39. "The Concept of Morality." *Journal of Philosophy* 63 (1966): 688–696.

40. "A Model for Analyzing a Philosophy of Education." *High School Journal* 2 (1966): 8–13.

41. "On Saying the Ethical Thing." *Proceedings and Addresses of the American Philosphical Association* 39 (1966): 21–42.

42. "Philosophical Enquiry." In *The Changing American School*, edited by John I. Goodlad, 1966, pp. 243–265 (Chapter X). The 65th Yearbook of the National Society for the Study of Education, Part II. Chicago: University of Chicago Press.

43. "G. H. von Wright on the Theory of Morals, Legislation and Value." *Ethics* 76 (1966): 131–136.

44. "J. D. Wild on Responsibility." *Philosophy and Phenomenological Research* 27 (1966): 90–96.

45. "Reply to Professor Wild." *Philosophy and Phenomenological Research* 27 (1966): 103.

46. "The Concept of Morality." *University of Colorado Studies in Philosophy*, No. 3 (1967): 1–22.

47. "Frondizi on the Foundations of Moral Norms." In *Proceedings of the Seventh Inter-American Congress of Philosophy*. Laval University Press, 1967, pp. 13–19.

48. "Value and Valuation." In *The Encyclopedia of Philosophy*, vol. 8, edited by Paul Edwards, pp. 229–232. New York: Macmillan and Free Press, 1967.

49. "Educational Values and Goals: Some Dispositions To Be Fostered." *Monist* 52 (1968): 1–10.

50. "Freedom: Responsibility and Decision." *Proceedings of the XIVth International Congress of Philosophy* 1 (1968): 143–154.

51. "Two Notes on Representation." In *Nomos X: Representation*, edited by Roland Pennock, pp. 49–51. New York: Atherton Press, 1968.

52. "War and the New Morality." *Reformed Journal* 18 (1968): 20–21.

53. "Ought and Is Once More." *Man and World* 2 (1969): 515–533.

54. "Educating for the Good Life." In *Prespectives in Education, Religion and the Arts*, edited by H. E. Kiefer and M. K. Munitz, pp. 17–42. Albany, New York: University of New York Press, 1970.

55. "A Model for Analyzing a Philosophy of Education." In *Readings in the Philosophy of Education: A Study of the Curriculum*, edited by J. R. Martin, pp. 15–22. Boston: Allyn and Bacon, 1970.

56. "Prichard and the Ethics of Virtue." *Monist* 54 (1970): 1–17.

57. "The Principles and Categories of Morality." In *Contemporary American Philosophy, Second Series*, edited by J. E. Smith, pp. 93–106. London: Allen and Unwin, 1970.

58. "Moral Education." In *The Encyclopedia of Education*, vol. 6, edited by L. C. Deighton, pp. 394–398. New York: Macmillan and Free Press, 1971.

59. "Philosophy of Education." In *The Encyclopedia of Education*, vol. 7, edited by L. C. Deighton, pp. 101–104. New York: Macmillan and Free Press, 1971.

60. "The Concept of Education Today." In *Educational Judgments*, edited by J. F. Doyle, pp. 19–32. London: Routledge and Kegan Paul, 1973.

61. "Education." In *Dictionary of the History of Ideas*, vol. 2, edited by P. P. Wiener, pp. 71–85. New York: Charles Scribner's Sons, 1973.

62. "The Ethics of Love Conceived as an Ethics of Virtue." *Journal of Religious Ethics* 1 (1973): 21–36.

63. "Is Morality Logically Dependent on Religion?" In *Religion and Morality*, edited by Gene Outka and John P. Reeder, pp. 195–317. Garden City, New York: Anchor Books, 1973.

64. "On Defining Moral Judgments, Principles, and Codes." *Etycka* 11 (1973): [In Polish.]

65. "The Principles of Morality." In *Skepticism and Moral Principles*, edited by C. L. Carter, pp. 43–76. Evanston, Illinois: New University Press, 1973.

66. "Under What Net?" *Philosophy* 48 (1973): 319–326.

67. "The Philosopher's Attack on Morality." *Philosophy* 49 (1974): 345–356.

68. "Sidgwick and the Dualism of Practical Reason." *Monist* 58 (1974): 449–467.

69. "Spinoza's 'New Morality': Notes on Book IV." In *Spinoza: Essays and Interpretation*, edited by Eugene Freeman and Maurice Mandelbaum, pp. 85–100. LaSalle, Illinois: Open Court Press, 1975.

70. "Conversations with Carney and Hauerwas." *Journal of Religious Ethics* 3 (1975): 45–62. Also includes complete bibliography of Frankena's writings.

71. "The Philosophy of Vocation." *Thought* 51 (1976): 393–408.

72. "Concluding More or Less Philosophical Postscript." In *Perspectives on Morality: Essays by William K. Frankena*, edited by K. E. Goodpaster, pp. 208–217. Notre Dame: University of Notre Dame Press, 1976.

73. "Some Beliefs About Justice." The Lindley Lecture, University of Kansas, 1966. In *Freedom and Morality*, edited by John Bricke, pp. 53–71. Lawrence: University of Kansas Press, 1976.

74. "The Ethics of Respect for Life." Thalheimer Lecture, Johns Hopkins University, 1975. In *Respect for Life*, edited by Stephen Barker, pp. 24–62. Baltimore: the Johns Hopkins University Press, 1977.

75. "Moral Philosophy and World Hunger." In *World Hunger and Moral Obligation*, edited by W. Aiken and H. La Follette, pp. 66–84. Englewood Cliffs, New Jersey: Prentice-Hall, Inc., 1977.

76. "Spinoza on the Knowledge of Good and Evil." *Philosophia* 7 (March 1977): 15–44.

77. "Ethics and the Environment." In *Ethics, The Environment and the Future*, edited by K. Sayre and K. E. Goodpaster, pp. 3–20. Notre Dame: University of Notre Dame Press, 1979.

78. "Methods of Ethics, 1977." *Ratio* 21 (December 1979): 125–134.

79. "Three Questions About Morality." The Carus Lectures for 1974 in *Monist* 63 (January 1980). (1) "Must Morality Have An Object," pp. 3–26; (2) "Is Morality A System of Ordinary Oughts," pp.

27–47; (3) "Has Morality An Independent Bottom," pp. 48–68. These lectures received critical comment by Alan Gewirth, G. J. Warnock, and Harald Ofstad. Professor Frankena responded to his critics in the same volume: "A Reply to My Three Critics," pp. 110–128.

80. "Is Morality a Purely Personal Matter?" In *Midwest Studies in Philosophy*, vol. III. Minneapolis: University of Minnesota Press, 1980, pp. 122–132.

II. CRITICAL COMMENT

Aiken, Henry David. "Contra—The Moral Point of View." *Philosophic Exchange* (Summer 1980): 57–79.

Brenkert, George G. "Frankena and Metaethical Absolutism." *Philosophical Studies* 34 (August 1978): 153–168.

Carney, Frederick. "On Frankena and Religious Ethics." *Journal of Religious Ethics* 3 (Spring 1975): 7–25.

Foot, Philippa. "A Reply to Professor Frankena." *Philosophy* 50 (October 1975): 455–459.

Gewirth, Alan. "Limitations of the Moral Point of View." *Monist* 63 (January 1980): 69–84.

Hauerwas, Stanley. "Obligation and Virtue Once More." *Journal of Religious Ethics* 3 (Spring 1975): 27–44.

Luebke, Neil R. "Frankena on the Naturalistic Fallacy." *Journal of Thought* 5 (October 1970): 262–272.

Ofstad, Harold. "Was Paradise Better?" *Monist* 63 (January 1980): 93–109.

Robbins, J. Wesley. "Frankena On The Difference Between An Ethic of Virtue And An Ethic of Duty." *Journal of Religious Ethics* 4 (Spring 1976): 57–62.

Schenck Jr., David. "Re-Casting The 'Ethics of Virtue/Ethics of Duty' Debate." *Journal of Religious Ethics* 4 (Fall 1976): 269–286.

Storer, Morris B. "Professor Frankena's Rendezvous With The Absolute." *Inquiry* 12 (Summer 69): 246–253.

Veatch, Henry. "Are There Non-Moral Goods." *New Scholasticism* 52 (Fall 1978): 471–499.

Warnock, G. J. "Comments on Frankena's Three Questions." *Monist* 63 (January 1980): 85–92.

Wheeler, Arthur M. "On 'The Principles of Morality'." *Journal of Value Inquiry* 13 (Winter 1979): 299–304.

III. RELATED BOOKS AND ARTICLES

Baier, Kurt. "The Point of View of Morality." *Australasian Journal of Philosophy* XXXII (1954): 104–135.

_____. *The Moral Point of View.* New York: Random House, 1965.

_____. "Moral Reasons and Reasons To Be Moral." In *Values and Morals*, edited by A. I. Goldman and J. Kim, pp. 231–253. Boston: D. Reidel Publishing Co., 1978. [Baier adopts a material account of the moral point of view. Much of his analysis focuses on why it is rational to take the moral point of view.]

Boatright, John R. "The Practicality of Moral Judgments." *Philosophical Quarterly* 23 (October 1973): 316–334. [Argues for an internalist position on the relation between motivation and obligation. The distinction between the internalist and the externalist on this question is Frankena's. See Frankena's "Obligation and Motivation in Recent Moral Philosophy."]

Falk, W. D. "Morality, Self and Others." In *Morality and the Language of Conduct*, edited by Hector-Neri Castaneda and George Naknikian, pp. 25–67. Detroit: Wayne State University Press, 1963. [Discusses whether duties to oneself are legitimate *moral* duties.]

Hare, R. M. *Freedom and Reason.* Oxford: The Clarendon Press, 1963. [The classic account of a formalist conception of the moral point of view.]

Quinton, Anthony. "The Bounds of Morality." In *Ethics and Social Justice*, edited by H. E. Kiefer and M. K. Munitz, pp. 122–141. Albany: State University of New York Press, 1970. [Argues for a material criterion based on diminishing suffering as the mark of the moral.]

Snare, Frank. "Three Sceptical Theses In Ethics." *American Philosophical Quarterly* 14 (April 1977): 129–136. [A critique of Frankena's position on the naturalistic fallacy.]

Strawson, P. F. "Social Morality and Individual Ideal." *Philosophy* XXXVI (1961): 1–17. [Tries to determine when socially sanctioned demands are genuine moral duties.]

Taylor, P. W. "On Taking The Moral Point of View." *Midwest Studies in Philosophy* III (1978): 35–61. [Analyzes the notions of (1) taking the moral point of view; (2) the criteria for classifying a principle as a moral principle; and (3) the conditions necessary for a moral principle to be binding on agents.]

Taylor, Paul. *Normative Discourse.* Englewood Cliffs, NJ: Prentice-Hall, Inc., 1961, pp. 107–150. [Taylor's analysis of what constitutes the moral point of view and his account of how such a point of view can be justified.]

Thornton, J. C. "Can the Moral Point of View be Justified." In *Readings in Contemporary Ethical Theory*, edited by Kenneth Pakel and M. Schiller, pp. 442–453. Englewood Cliffs, NJ: Prentice-Hall, Inc., 1970. [Shows how discussions about the moral point of view quickly lead to "Why be moral?" questions.]

Wallace, G. and Walker, A. D. M. (eds.), *The Definition of Morality*. London: Methuen & Co. Ltd., 1970. [This anthology covers a broader range of issues than defining "the moral point of view." See particularly the article by Strawson (cited above) and the two articles by Neil Cooper.]

Richard B. Brandt

I. PUBLICATIONS

Books

1. *The Philosophy of Schleiermacher*, viii and 350. New York: Harper and Brothers, 1941.

2. *Hopi Ethics: A Theoretical Analysis*, viii and 386. Chicago: University of Chicago Press, 1954.

3. *Ethical Theory*, viii and 528. Englewood Cliffs, New Jersey: Prentice-Hall, 1959.

4. *Value and Obligation: Systematic Readings in Ethics*, vi and 707. New York: Harcourt Brace, 1961.

5. (Editor) *Social Justice*, vi and 169. Englewood Cliffs, New Jersey: Prentice-Hall, 1962.

6. (Co-editor, with Ernest Nagel) *Meaning and Knowledge: Systematic Readings in Epistemology*. New York: Harcourt, Brace and World, xiv and 668, 1964.

7. (Co-editor, with W. P. Alston) *The Problems of Philosophy: Introductory Readings*. Boston: Allyn and Bacon, 1966, 704 pp.

8. *A Theory of the Good and the Right*. Oxford: Clarendon Press, 1979.

9. *Thinking About Morality*. Ann Arbor: University of Michigan Press, 1980.

Articles

1. "On the Possibility of Reference to Inferred Entities." *Journal of*

Philosophy 35 (1938): 393–405.

2. "An Emotional Theory of the Judgment of Moral Worth." *Ethics* 52 (1941): 41–79.

3. "The Significance of Differences of Ethical Opinion for Ethical Rationalism." *Philosophy and Phenomenological Research* 4 (1944): 469–494.

4. "Moral Valuation." *Ethics* 56 (1946): 106–121.

5. "The Emotive Theory of Ethics." *Philosophical Review* 59 (1950): 305–318.

6. "Stevenson's Defense of the Emotive Theory." *Philosophical Review* 59 (1950): 535–540.

7. "A Criterion of Necessity." *Review of Metaphysics* 6 (1952): 125–126.

8. "The Status of Empirical Assertion Theories in Ethics." *Mind* 61 (1952): 458–479.

9. "Thinking and Experience." *Review of Metaphysics* 7 (1954): 632–643.

10. "Knowledge and Certainty." *Review of Metaphysics* 7 (1954): 682–684.

11. "The Definition of an 'Ideal Observer' Theory in Ethics." *Philosophy and Phenomenological Research* 15 (1954): 407–413.

12. "Comments on Professor Firth's Reply." *Philosophy and Phenomenological Research* 15 (1954): 422–423.

13. "A Puzzle in Lewis' Theory of Memory." *Philosophical Studies* 5 (1954): 88–95.

14. "The Epistemological Status of Memory Beliefs." *Philosophical Review* 64 (1955): 78–95.

15. "Philip Blair Rice on Ethical Theory." *Philosophy and Phenomenological Research* 17 (1957): 404–411.

16. "The Languages of Realism and Nominalism." *Philosophy and Phenomenological Research* 17 (1957): 516–535.

17. "Some Puzzles for Attitude Theories of Value." In *The Language of Value*, edited by R. Lepley, pp. 153–177. New York: Columbia University Press, 1957, and "Response to Stevenson's Comments," *ibid.*, pp. 323–325.

18. "Blameworthiness and Obligation." In *Essays in Moral Philosophy*, edited by A. I. Melden, pp. 3–39. Seattle: University of Washington Press, 1958.

19. Articles on "Duty" and "Ethics" in *Encyclopedia Americana*.

20. "Determinism and the Justifiability of Moral Blame." In *Deter-*

minism and Freedom, edited by Sidney Hook, pp. 137–143. New York: New York University Press, 1958.

21. "The Conditions of Criminal Responsibility." *Nomos* 3 (1960): 106–115.

22. "Doubts About the Identity Theory." In *Dimensions of Mind*, edited by Sidney Hook, pp. 57–67. New York: New York University Press, 1960.

23. "Toward a Credible Form of Utilitarianism." In *Morality and the Language of Conduct*, edited by H. N. Castaneda and G. Nakhnikian, pp. 107–143. Detroit: Wayne State University Press, 1963.

24. "Personality Traits as Causal Explanations in Biography." In *Philosophy and History*, edited by S. Hook, pp. 192–204. New York: New York University Press, 1963.

25. *Moral Philosophy and the Analysis of Language*. The Lindley Lecture, published in the Department of Philosophy. Lawrence: University of Kansas, 1963, pp. 1–24.

26. (Co-author, with Jaegwon Kim) "Wants as Explanations of Actions." *Journal of Philosophy* LX (1963): 425–435.

27. "The Concepts of Obligation and Duty." *Mind* LXXIII (1964): 374–393.

28. "Utility and the Obligation to Obey the Law." In *Law and Philosophy*, edited by Sidney Hook. New York: New York University Press, 1964.

29. "Epistemic Priority and Coherence." *Journal of Philosophy* LXI (1964): 557–559.

30. "Critique of MacIntyre's Starting-Point." In *Faith and the Philosophers*, edited by John Hick, pp. 150–153. New York: St. Martin's Press, Inc., 1964.

31. "The Concept of Welfare." In *The Structure of Economic Science: Essays on Methodology*, edited by S. R. Krupp, pp. 257–276. Englewood Cliffs, New Jersey: Prentice-Hall, Inc., 1966.

32. "Personal Values and the Justification of Institutions." In *Human Values and Economic Policy*, edited by Sidney Hook, pp. 22–40. New York: New York University Press, 1967.

33. (Co-author, with Jaegwon Kim) "The Logic of the Identity Theory." *Journal of Philosophy* LXIV (1967): 515–537.

34. "Some Merits of One Form of Rule-utilitarianism." *University of Colorado Studies in Philosophy* 1967: 39–65.

35. Articles in the *Encyclopedia of Philosophy*, edited by Paul Edwards. New York: Macmillan and Free Press, 8 vols.; on Hedonism;

Ethical Relativism; Emotive Theory of Ethics; Epistemology and Ethics, The Parallel Between.

36. "A Utilitarian Theory of Excuses." *Philosophical Review* 78 (1969): 337–361.

37. "Traits of Character: A Conceptual Analysis." *American Philosophical Quarterly* 7 (1970): 23–37.

38. "Rational Desires." *Proceedings and Addresses, The American Philosophical Association* (Presidential Address, Western Division) XLIII (1970): 43–64.

39. "Comment on MacCallum." *Inquiry* 14 (1971): 314–317.

40. "Comment on Kaufman." *Inquiry* 14 (1971): 207–212.

41. "Utilitarianism and the Rules of War." *Philosophy and Public Affairs*, vol. 2 (1972): 145–165.

42. "The Morality of Abortion." *The Monist* 56, No. 4 (1972): 503–526.

43. "Rationality, Egoism, and Morality." *The Journal of Philosophy* 69 (1972): 681–697.

44. "Should the Choice of a Moral System Be Impartial?" *Etyka* (Warsaw) XI (1973): 57–85.

45. "The Morality of Abortion." Revised version, In *Abortion: Pro and Con*, edited by R. L. Perkins, pp. 151–172. Cambridge, Massachusetts: Schenkman Publishing Corp., 1974.

46. "A Moral Principle About Killing." In *Beneficent Euthanasia*, edited by Marvin Kohl. Buffalo: Prometheus Books, 1975.

47. "The Morality and Rationality of Suicide." In *A Handbook for the Study of Suicide*, edited by Edwin Schneidman, pp. 61–76. Fair Lawn, New Jersey: Oxford Press, 1975. Reprinted in enlarged and revised form in *Suicidology: Contemporary Developments*, edited by Edwin Schneidman, pp. 378–399. New York: Grune and Stratton, 1975.

48. "The Psychology of Benevolence and Its Implications for Philosophy." *Journal of Philosophy* 78 (1976): 429–453.

49. "The Concept of Rationality in Ethical and Political Theory." In *Nomos XVII, Human Nature in Politics*, edited by Pennock and Chapman, pp. 265–79. 1977.

50. "Defective Newborns and the Morality of Termination." In *Infanticide and the Value of Life*, edited by Marvin Kohl, pp. 46–60. Buffalo: Prometheus Books, 1978.

51. "Case Studies in Bioethics: A Suicide Attempt and Emergency

Room Ethics, A Commentary." *Hastings Center Report* 9 (August 1979): 12–13.

52. "Is Ethics a Science?" *Zygon* 15 (March 1980): 21–28.

53. "Moral Principles Relevant to Euthanasia." In *Ethics, Humanism and Medicine*, edited by Marc D. Basson, pp. 43–50. New York: Liss, 1980.

II. CRITICAL COMMENT

Foulk, Gary J. "Brandt and the Concept of Human Rights." *Southwest Journal of Philosophy* 4 (Summer 1973): 39–42.

Gautier, David P. "Brandt on Egoism." *Journal of Philosophy* 69 (November 1972): 697–698.

Gibbard, Allan F. "Rule Utilitarianism: Merely an Illusory Alternative." *Australasian Journal of Philosophy* 43 (August 1965): 211–20.

Hare, William F. "A Mixed Form of the Summary Theory of Character-Traits Defined." *Personalist* 52 (Autumn 1971): 750–754.

Harrod, R. F. "Utilitarianism Revised." *Mind* 45 (1936): 137–56. [Harrod's form of rule-utilitarianism was criticized by Brandt but was defended against Brandt's attack by Gibbard (see #3 above) —Ed.]

Hudson, Stephen D. "Character Traits and Desires." *Ethics* 90 (July 1980): 539–549.

Johnson, Conrad D. "Brandt's Ideally Rational Moral Legislation." *Social Theory and Practice*, vol. 7, No. 2 (Summer 1981): 205–221.

Loftin, Robert W. "An Inconsistency In Brandt's Ethical Theory." *Personalist* 51 (Fall 1970): 486–489.

Nielsen, Kai. "Covert and Overt Synonymity: Brandt and Moore and the 'Naturalistic Fallacy'." *Philosophical Studies* 25 (January 1974): 51–56.

Overvold, Mark Carl. "Self Interest and the Concept of Self-Sacrifice." *Canadian Journal of Philosophy* 10 (March 1980): 105–118.

Sankowski, Edward T. "The Sense of Responsibility and the Justifiability of Emotion." *Southern Journal of Philosophy* 13 (Summer 1975): 215–233.

Schlecht, Ludwig F. "Universalizability and the Impartiality of Brandt's Ideal Observer." *Philosophical Forum* 2 (Spring 1971): 396–401.

Shope, Robert K. "Rawls, Brandt, and the Definition of Rational Desires." *Canadian Journal of Philosophy* 8 (June 1978): 329–340.

Sobel, "Rule Utilitarianism." *Australasian Journal of Philosophy* 46 (1968): 146–65.

Wall, George B. "More On The Equivalence of Act and Rule Utilitarianism." *Philosophical Studies* 22 (Oct.–Dec. 71): 91–95.

Weiss, Donald D. "An Incredible Utilitarianism." *Journal of Value Inquiry* 8 (Winter 1975): 308–312.

Reviews of *A Theory of The Good and The Right*:

Cohen, Brenda. *Philosophical Quarterly* 30 (July 1980): 271–73.

Emmet, Dorothy. *Philosophy* 55 (July 1980): 412–414.

Mitchell, Dorothy. *Philosophical Books* 21 (October 1980): 223–229.

III. RELATED BOOKS AND ARTICLES

Feinberg, Joel. "The Forms and Limits of Utilitarianism." *Philosophical Review* 76 (1967): 368–381. [A discussion of Lyons' work on the equivalence of act and "general" utilitarianism.]

Harrison, Jonathan. "Utilitarianism, Univeralization, and Our Duty To Be Just." Aristotelian Society Proceedings Vol. 53 (1952–53): 105–34. [Considers the objection as to whether utilitarianism requires that one *always* be doing the most benevolent action.]

Haslett, David W. *Moral Rightness*. The Hague: Martinus Nijhoff, 1974). [A contemporary rule-utilitarian position inspired by C. I. Lewis.]

Lyons, David. *Forms and Limits of Utilitarianism*. Oxford: Clarendon Press, 1965. [A detailed study which shows that rule utilitarianism cannot establish its superiority to act utilitarianism.]

Narveson, Jan. *Morality and Utility*. Baltimore: Johns Hopkins Press, 1967.

Rawls, John. "Two Concepts of Rules." *Philosophical Review* vol. 64 (1955): 3–32. [The closest Rawls comes to a utilitarian position. He defends a variation of rule utilitarianism. Compare this piece with his discussion of utilitarianism in *A Theory of Justice*.]

Sartorius, Rolf E. *Individual Conduct and Social Norms: A Utilitarian Account of Social Union and the Rule of Law*. Encino, CA: Dickinsen Publishing Company, Inc., 1975. [Innovative defenses of act utilitarianism.]

Smart, J. J. C. "Extreme and Restricted Utilitarianism." *Philosophical Quarterly* vol. 6 (1956): 344–354.

_____. *An Outline of Utilitarian Ethics*. Melbourne: Melbourne University Press, 1961.

_____ and Bernard Williams. *Utilitarianism: For and Against*. (Cambridge, England: Cambridge University Press, 1973. [One of the best head-to-head debates between a utilitarian and a deontologist.]

[J. J. C. Smart is the best known contemporary defender of act utilitarianism—a position defended in all three citations above.]

"Symposium: The Consequences of Actions." *Aristotelian Society Supplement* 30 (1956), 2 articles, A. N. Prior and D. D. Raphael: 91–119. [Prior argues that it is logically impossible to discover what one's duty is when doing one's duty is acting to bring about the best consequences. Professor Raphael criticizes Prior's analysis.]

Abraham I. Melden

I. PUBLICATIONS

Books

1. (Editor). *Ethical Theories.* New York: Prentice-Hall. First edition, 1950; Second edition, 1955; Second edition; Revised 1967.

2. *Rights and Right Conduct.* Oxford: Basil Blackwell, 1959. Reprinted New York: Humanities Press and Oxford: Basil Blackwell, 1970.

3. (Editor). *Essays in Moral Philosophy.* Seattle: University of Washington, 1958.

4. (Editor and Introductory Essay). A. E. Murphy, *The Theory of Practical Reason.* La Salle, Illinois: Open Court, 1964.

5. *Free Action.* London: Routledge & Kegan Paul, and New York: Humanities Press, 1961.

6. (Editor). *Human Rights.* Belmont, California: Wadsworth, 1970.

7. *Rights and Persons.* Oxford: Basil Blackwell and Berkeley: University of California Press, 1977.

Articles

1. "Thought and Its Objects." *Philosophy of Science*, October 1940: 434–441.

2. "Judgments in the Social Sciences." *University of California Publications in Philosophy*, 1942: 133–158.

3. "On the Method of Ethics." *Journal of Philosophy*, March 1948: 169–181.

4. "Why Be Moral?" *Journal of Philosophy*, August 1948: 449–456.

5. "Two Comments on Utilitarianism." *The Philosophical Review*, October 1951: 508–524.

6. "The Concept of Universal Human Rights." In *Language, Science and Human Rights*. Philadelphia: University of Pennsylvania Press, 1952: pp. 167–188.

7. "Historical Objectivity—A Noble Dream?" *Journal of General Education*, October 1952: 17–24.

8. "The Obligation to Keep a Promise." *Proc. of the 11th International Congress of Philosophy*, vol. 10 (1953), pp. 153–158.

9. "On Promising." *Mind*, January 1958: 49–66.

10. "Action." *The Philosophical Review*, October 1956: 523–541.

11. "My Kinaesthetic Sensations Advise Me." *Analysis* XVIII (1957-8): 43–48.

12. "British Philosophy in the Mid-Century." *Philosophy* No. 34 (1959): 28–37.

13. "Willing." *The Philosophical Review*, October 1960: 475–484.

14. "Le Posizione Sociale dei Diritti e Degle Obblighi Morali." *Revista di Filosofia* LII, July 1962: 243–263.

15. "Reasons for Action and Matters of Fact." Presidential Address, American Philosophical Association, Pacific Division, *Proc. of the American Philos. Assoc.*, vol. XXXV, October 1962, pp. 45–60.

16. "Désir et Action." *Les Etudes Philosophiques* No. 3, 1964, pp. 347–360.

17. "Utility and Moral Reasoning." In *Ethics and Society*, edited by R. T. De George, pp. 173–196. New York: Doubleday and Company, Anchor Books, 1966.

18. "Desires as Causes of Action." In *Current Philosophical Issues*, edited by F. C. Dommeyer, pp. 127–150. Springfield, Illinois: Chas C. Thomas, 1966.

19. "Philosophy and the Understanding of Human Fact." In *New Essays in Epistemology*, edited by Avrum Stroll, pp. 229–249. New York: Harper and Row, 1967.

20. "The Conceptual Dimensions of Emotions." In *Human Action*, edited by T. Mischel, pp. 199–221. New York: Academic Press, 1969.

21. "Expressives, Descriptives, Performatives." *Philosophy and Phe-*

nomenological Research vol. XXIX, No. 4, June 1969: 498–505.

22. "Rejoinder to Viullemin." In *Language and Human Nature*, edited by Paul Kurtz, pp. 18–26. St. Louis: Warren H. Green, Inc.

23. "Moral Education and Moral Action." In *Moral Education*, edited by C. M. Beck, B. X. Crittenden and E. V. Sullivan. Toronto: University of Toronto Press, 1971.

24. "Willing and the Will: A Rejoinder." *Philosophy and Phenomenological Research*, vol. XXXI, March, 1971: 451–453.

25. "Olafson on Education." In *Educational Judgments: Papers in the Philosophy of Education*, edited by James Doyle, pp. 196–206. London: Routledge & Kegan Paul, 1972.

26. "The Play of Rights," invited essay. *The Monist*, Oct. 1972: 479–502.

27. "Do Infants Have Moral Rights?" In *Children's Rights: Moral Essays on Developing Persons*, edited by William Aiken and Hugh La Follette. Totowa, NJ: Littlefield and Adams, 1980.

28. "Are There Welfare Rights?" In *Income Support: Conceptual Policy Issues*, edited by Peter G. Brown, Conrad Johnson and Paul Vernier. Totowa, NJ: Roman and Littlefield, 1981.

II. CRITICAL COMMENT

Davis, Lawrence H. "Actions." *Canadian Journal of Philosophy*, Supp. 1 (1974): 129–144.

Machan, Tibor R. "Some Recent Work on Human Rights Theory." *American Philosophical Quarterly* 17 (April 1980): 103–115.

Owens, Meirlys. "The Notion of Human Rights: A Reconsideration." *American Philosophical Quarterly* 6 (July 1969): 240–246.

Radford, Robert T. "Logical Relations and Causal Relations." *Personalist* 52 (Autumn 1971): 599–617.

Schoedinger, Andrew B. *Wants, Decisions and Human Actions: A Praxeological Investigation*. Washington, D.C.: University Press of America, 1978.

White, Stephen W. "The Equality Principle: Is It Linguistically Justifiable?" *Personalist* 55 (Winter 1974): 53–60.

Wilkins, Burleigh T. "Melden on Willing." *Philosophy and Phenomenological Research* 31 (March 1971): 444–450.

Reviews of *Rights and Persons*

Boyle Jr., Joseph M. *Thomist* 45 (April 1981): 332–33.

Britton, Karl. *Philosophy* 54 (January 1979): 122–25.

Cohen, Brenda. *Philosophical Quarterly* 28 (October 1978): 371–73.

Lindley, Richard. *Mind* 88 (July 1979): 464–466.

Mahowald, Mary B. *Philosophy and Phenomenological Research.* (September 1979): 139–140.

Martin, Rex. *Review of Metaphysics* 33 (March 1980): 642–645.

Mendus, S. L. *Philosophical Books* (October 1978): 136–137.

III. RELATED BOOKS AND ARTICLES

Dworkin, Ronald. *Taking Rights Seriously.* Cambridge, MA: Harvard University Press, 1977. [Rights as trumps against utilitarian consideration.]

Feinberg, Joel. "Duties, Rights, and Claims." *American Philosophical Quarterly* 3 (1966): 137–44.

————. "The Nature and Value of Rights." *Journal of Value Inquiry* IV (Winter 1970): 243–57.

————. *Social Philosophy*, chapters 4–6. Englewood Cliffs, NJ: Prentice Hall, 1973. [Feinberg's work carefully develops the entitlement theory of rights.]

Fried, Charles. *Right and Wrong*, chapters 4–6. Cambridge, MA: Harvard University Press, 1978. [Argues that the theory of rights must be built upon a theory of right and wrong.]

Gewirth, Alan. *Reason and Morality.* Chicago: University of Chicago Press, 1978. [A sophisticated, technical, and controversial attempt to ground human (generic) rights logically in the features of human action.]

Hart, H.L.A. "Are There Any Natural Rights?" *The Philosophical Review* LXIV (April 1955): 175–191. [Defends the claim that if there are any rights at all, there must be a natural right to liberty.]

Hohfeld, Wesley Newcomb. *Fundamental Legal Conceptions.* New Haven: Yale University Press, 1946. [A classic attempt at definition.]

"Human Rights." *The Monist* 52 (1968). [See particularly the analyses of Arnold S. Kaufman and W. T. Blackstone.]

MacDonald, Margaret. "Natural Rights." *Proceedings of the Aristotelian Society* 47 (1946–47): 225–50. [Equal natural rights claims cannot be based on natural characteristics of humans.]

Mackie, John L. "Can There Be A Rights-Based Moral Theory?" *Midwest Studies In Philosophy* 3 (1978).

Macklin, Ruth. "Moral Concerns and Appeals to Rights and Duties." *The Hastings Center Report* 6 (1976): 31–38.

McCloskey, H. J. "Rights." *Philosophical Quarterly* 15 (1965): 115–127.

Montague, Philip. "Two Concepts of Rights." *Philosophy and Public Affairs* 9 (Summer 1980): 372–384. [Analyzes the conceptual link between having a right and being capable of intentional activity.]

Pennock, J. Roland and John W. Chapman (eds.). *Human Rights.* Nomos XXIII. New York: New York University Press, 1981. [An entire Nomos volume focusing on rights. Articles by John Charvet and Frithjof Bergmann consider whether a theory of rights can be based on human nature. Conceptual issues concerning the scope of human rights are discussed by Kurt Baier and William N. Nelson.]

Simon, Robert L. In *The Individual and The Political Order* by Norman E. Bowie and Robert L. Simon, chapter III. Englewood Cliffs, NJ: Prentice-Hall Inc., 1977. [Rights are presupposed if people are to be treated as full moral persons.]

Singer, Marcus G. "The Basis of Rights and Duties." *Philosophical Studies* 23 (1972): 48–57.

Vlastos, Gregory. "Justice and Equality." In *Social Justice*, edited by Richard Brandt, pp. 31–72. Englewood Cliffs, NJ: Prentice-Hall Inc., 1962. [Defends the claim that we have equal rights to liberty and well-being.]

Wasserstrom, Richard A. "Rights, Human Rights and Racial Discrimination." *Journal of Philosophy* 61 (1964): 628-641. [An analysis of the nature and scope of human rights.]